A GUIDE TO
CASTLES
IN BRITAIN
Where to find them and what to look for

A GUIDE TO
CASTLES
IN BRITAIN

Where to find them and what to look for
PHILIP WARNER

NEW ENGLISH LIBRARY
TIMES MIRROR

First published in Great Britain by New English Library
Limited, Barnard's Inn, Holborn, London EC1N 2JR in
1976. This edition, completely revised and enlarged,
published in 1981

Design: Ian Hughes

Typeset by Photobooks (Bristol) Ltd, Bristol

Printed and bound by
Butler and Tanner Ltd, Frome, Somerset

ISBN: 0–450–04833–0

The publishers would like to thank the following
individuals and organisations for their kind permission
to reproduce photographs in this book:
Aerofilms Limited 40, 54–55, 63, 64, 78, 107, 109, 123,
    181, 187
David Beardwell 80
British Tourist Authority 57, 74–75, 79, 90–91, 118–119,
    122, 130, 138–139, 148, 162–163, 165, 167, 168–169,
    173, 185
Crown Copyright 44, 61, 67, 112, 161, 178, 183
Gillian Dark 50, 127
Robert Gray 35
Robert Herd 146
Jon Hirons 177
Duncan Hughes 70
Ian Hughes 41, 42, 43, 51, 69, 104, 115, 120, 128, 129,
    134, 135, 136, 150, 151, 152, 157
Peter Lidbury 106
New English Library 179
Photo Precision Limited 34, 59, 68, 73, 85, 111, 131, 153,
    154, 171
Popperfoto 52, 53, 84, 88, 99, 142
Philip Warner 81, 101, 108, 110, 144, 145, 149, 175

CONTENTS

INTRODUCTION

Increasing numbers of people are fascinated by castles. Some of these 'castle-hunters' are British but many come from overseas. When you visit a 'busy' castle you are likely to find Americans, French, Germans, Dutch and many other nationalities among the visitors. Almost every country in the world has castles: in some they are well maintained, in others neglected. The Germans have an excellent attitude, and whenever possible they put an attractive restaurant in or near the main building. Fortunately, this custom is spreading and there are a number of castles in England where the visitor can obtain refreshment.

Better still, there are castles in Britain where you can stay and feel as if you were the hereditary owner. There are castles where you can enjoy a medieval feast, complete with buxom wenches and bawdy humour. There are castles where you may eat to the highest standard possible, but not cheaply. There are castles where you may be scared out of your wits ghost-hunting, or where you may give yourself nightmares – if you enjoy that sort of thing.

For most people, a castle is somewhere to go to in the car as an outing; somewhere to take some photographs; something with a touch of local, or even sinister, history; somewhere to excite young children. Sadly to say, if there is a guide-book on sale at the castle it is likely to be too technical and compressed for the visitors' needs. Many people thus fail to get the best out of their visit. The purpose of this book is to help people to enjoy visiting and exploring castles.

When you visit a castle you may wonder whether your ancestors lived in one and, if so, what their status was. Many of them certainly did live in a castle and members of your family might have been with them and have had a variety of posts from the highest to the lowest. The story is interesting. As your ancestry goes further back so the population becomes smaller. For example, in 1066 the population was probably less than a million: now it is fifty-five millions. This means that the network of your relations as they stretch back becomes closely interwoven with other people's. It is said, and probably rightly, that if your family has been living in this country since the eleventh century you are probably related thirteen times over to every duke, earl, baron, knight and peasant of that time by now. So, when you gaze over the battlements you may be standing exactly where one of your ancestors looked down at his peasants toiling in the field below. But one of those peasants may have been one of your ancestors, too; and perhaps that figure on the battlements fell in status during the next hundred years through bad luck, bad judgement or bad friends. In the same time the peasant may have risen; some families kept much the same status over hundreds of years, but they were a minority.

When you go to look at what may have been *your* castle – for even if you did not own it you belonged to it just as you belong to a school, a town or perhaps a regiment – there are many things to interest you. Very soon you may find yourself becoming an expert and able to understand why a castle is sited where it is, why it was built in a particular form, and what living inside it must have been like.

In Britain there are four main types of castle, though many buildings which do not deserve the name are still known as 'castles'. Many of these wrongly named edifices are pre-historic forts, mostly belonging to the middle and later Iron Age – from about 700 BC to Roman times. They are well worth a visit, and you may be very impressed by some of them. Maiden Castle, in Dorset, is a huge enclosure defended by high banks and deep ditches. The labour required to dig those ditches and raise those banks with primitive tools can hardly be imagined, but our early ancestors never avoided a task because it was difficult. The toil involved in transporting bluestones from South Wales to Stonehenge might have daunted a weak-willed person but it did not daunt our forebears. There are many early earthworks in Britain – none of them as large as Maiden Castle but all interesting and all worth a visit.

Our four categories of castle are:
Roman castles;
Motte and bailey castles;
Medieval stone castles and their successors;
Later residential castles.

Roman castles

Some people say that Roman castles are not castles at all but merely forts. A fort is generally understood to be a military strongpoint which is garrisoned but is not a residence. Forts tend to be squat and uncomfortable; in order to make them as defensible as possible they have few openings for light and air and the approaches are difficult. Roman forts (or castles) are usually spacious areas surrounded by high walls in which families could live for long periods. Nobody but a hermit could wish to live in an ordinary fort. We shall therefore treat Roman forts as early forms of castles and, we hope, encourage you to visit them.

Motte and bailey castles

There are several thousand motte and bailey castles in Britain. They were chiefly introduced at the Norman Conquest, though a few were built here even before 1066. The Normans found them a very successful device for consolidating the conquest of land, and creating a springboard for capturing more. The technique was simple but very effective. The Norman soldiers rounded up as many of the local people as they could find and set them to work building an earth mound. This was called a motte because that was the Norman word for turf. The motte was usually about 50 feet high and had steep sides. Around the base was a ditch which had been created by the removal of much of the earth taken to build the motte. This ditch would then be filled with water, if available, or with sharp stakes if the area was dry. Either way, the ditch was a formidable obstacle which an invader had to overcome before he could climb up the motte. Later the ground around the base was enclosed with a palisade of stakes and this was the bailey. Outside this palisade there might be another ditch. The bailey was used for enclosing minor buildings or, in time of danger, cattle and sheep.

On top of the motte, around the edges, was another palisade which was usually interlaced with sharp thorns. Normally, an attacker would try to set this on fire before he attempted to get through it. Nine hundred years later there is no significant trace of such wooden palisades which on some mottes were replaced by a stone wall, creating what came to be known as a shell-keep.

On the summit of the motte was a wooden tower of two or three storeys. The owner of the castle lived at the top, and the soldiers below, but it was all extremely uncomfortable and movement from one floor to another was by means of ladders. All cooking, of course, took place out of doors, and this must have made life

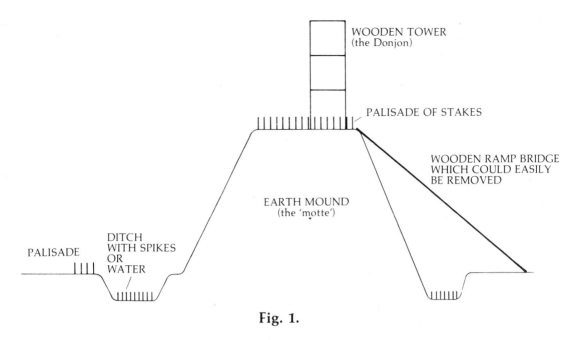

Fig. 1.

Fig 1: A motte. If the motte was enclosed in a wider palisade it became known as a motte and bailey castle.

difficult in rain, high wind, or snow. This tower was known as the donjon, and later was called the keep. As soon as the owner felt it was safe to do so he ceased to live in the donjon, which was then used for holding prisoners. Thus the underground dungeon originated well above ground, and the word motte survives now as the name of the ditch – the moat.

The Normans were a resourceful people and made the best use of materials to hand. When they came across an ancient earthwork – as at Thetford in Norfolk – they adapted that as a motte. The motte at Thetford is, incidentally, the tallest in Britain, being 120 feet high. They also used convenient crags. Where timber was scarce they built in stone from the beginning, but, of course, this had to be at ground level as a newly raised motte would not take the weight of stone. After about fifty years it was thought that some mottes had settled down firmly enough to take a stone donjon. Occasionally this worked, but – more often than not – the stone building began to lean and soon collapsed. The Normans were quick to appreciate that a stone donjon on level ground can be made a formidable defence if it is sturdy enough, and the White Tower of the Tower of London is typical of the massive buildings they erected to this end.

Some of the early castles were cunningly sited in the one dry spot in the middle of a marsh and these were very formidable indeed. One method of capturing a castle was to tunnel underneath it and bring down part of a wall. However, if as soon as you begin to tunnel water seeps into the diggings and fills them up, there is little point in continuing. Nowadays, when the countryside has been drained, it may be difficult at first to see why a castle was sited where it was; it may perhaps look quite vulnerable. However, if you look at the soil, the vegetation and the general lie of the land, a very different picture of the strategic possibilities will emerge.

INTRODUCTION

Motte and bailey castles continued to be built for several hundred years after the Normans arrived here, and often when you see the sign for a castle marked on a map, and go to find that castle, you will find a motte and bailey. As you clamber up the slope you may pause and wonder what it must have been like to do so under a hail of arrows and a shower of other missiles. You will be astonished to note how far you can see from the top of a motte, even in its present weather-worn state – which makes it much lower than when it was built – and without the donjon which gave extra height. Not only can you see a long way but you can also see all the places which matter – the courses of rivers, fords, entrances to valleys, and a long way into them. We are inclined to think of the Normans as fairly primitive but there was nothing amateurish about their strategic and tactical skills; the siting of their castles commands admiration today. There is a peculiar fascination in visiting motte and bailey castles, remote and inaccessible though some of them are. You feel you are in close touch with those tough old Normans. You are seeing the scene as they saw it.

Medeival stone castles and their successors

As we have already seen, building in stone began very soon after the Norman Conquest. There was nothing skimpy about the way the Normans tackled their building problems – they even imported high-quality stone from Caen, in Normandy, for use in some castles. As most of the early Norman stone castles are now ruins – the White Tower is, of course, an exception – it is not always easy to appreciate Norman building skills. It is, therefore, a good idea to visit Norman buildings which are well preserved and these are, of course, cathedrals. A visit to Durham or Ely Cathedral, for example, affords a good example of Norman architectural skills.

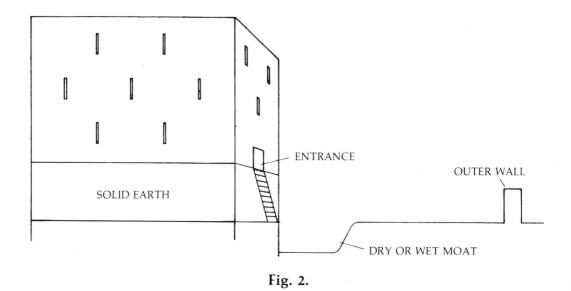

Fig. 2.

Fig 2: An early stone castle. The base was packed with solid earth and the entrance was by ladder or stairway to the floor above. Note the square corners and the lack of battlements. The slits in the walls were designed for light and ventilation.

But in the early stone castles the Normans were not trying to be architecturally clever, they were simply building for strength. Many of their keeps had no entrance at ground-floor level and the whole of the first floor was solid earth. Later, the solid earth first floor was sometimes hollowed out to make store-rooms but these could be approached only from above, within the castle. The walls of the building were immensely thick, sometimes as much as 20 feet, and the castles were solid and square, dark and uncomfortable. They looked impregnable but they were not.

The problem with any new weapon is that, as soon as it is in use, someone finds a way to combat it. This applies equally to whether it is an attacking or defending weapon. The Normans built their massive castles but their opponents – sometimes other Normans – soon realised that square castles were vulnerable at the corners where heavy stones slung from huge catapults could weaken the structure where the walls joined. Furthermore, surface miners could pick away at a lower level or even batter a piece off with a ram made from the trunk of a tree and propelled by about sixty men. Most dangerous of all, though slow, were the underground miners who would tunnel beneath the walls, make a large cavern, fill it with brushwood soaked in fat and then set light to it. The great heat created by this conflagration would usually crack the wall above – which now had no foundations – and might well bring down the entire corner structure. At Rochester you can still see where and how this was done; at St Andrews you can go into one of these underground mines.

Once the Normans had appreciated the weakness of square corners, they took steps to make them stronger. The obvious move was to replace the right angle by round towers whose curving surface would cause missiles to glance off and be difficult to hack away with a pick. After a while it was realised that if circular towers were also put in the centre of the side walls, they would enable an archer to direct his arrows accurately at anyone attempting to interfere with the corner towers. So the second stage of castle building, in the twelfth century, brought the introduction of these flanking towers which are often known as bastion towers.

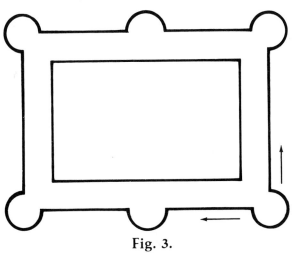

Fig. 3.

Fig 3: Making the castle less vulnerable. Round towers at the corners made these points less vulnerable, and enabled defenders to shoot along the walls.

INTRODUCTION

For a long time all defence was conducted from the battlements. In the eleventh century this had been a dangerous activity, for the defender was fully exposed and not always able to see clearly what was going on below. Soon, however, the designers turned their attention to the battlements which became crenellated – resembling teeth with wide gaps between them. The solid part was called the merlon and the gap was called the embrasure. However, dodging behind the merlon when the battlements were under heavy assault from arrows and slung stones (very effective and accurate), was not always successful, and a better device was soon introduced. These were hanging shutters, like a trap-door opening outwards. The defender pushed it open and sent off his own missile from behind this partial protection. A few of these old shutters have now been restored, but in most castles today you will find the only signs of their former presence are the grooves cut in the sides of the merlon; these took the hingeing arrangements.

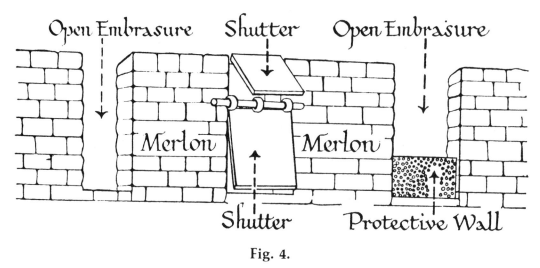

Fig. 4.

Fig 4: Battlements gave shelter to the defenders. The solid portion was known as the merlon and the open portion as the embrasure. Wooden shutters over the embrasure gave further protection.

Later still a more sophisticated device was developed to enable those on the battlements to attend to the problems created by opponents assaulting the lower walls. These were called hoardings or brattices. They were wooden structures, suspended from the top of the walls, rather like giant packing-cases, in which the occupants must have felt highly vulnerable, in spite of the wooden walls. The object of these contraptions was to enable missiles to be dropped directly onto those below. The missiles included heavy stones and quicklime. Anyone who looked upwards while trying to climb a ladder would be likely to find his eyes and clothing full of agonising quicklime. By the early thirteenth century most of the wooden brattices had been replaced by permanent stone structures, known as machicolations – which you can walk along today in many castles. As stone machicolations were fireproof, the missiles used by the defenders now included red-hot iron bars, red-hot sand, boiling water and fat. The labour involved in carrying sand and water to the battlements and then heating it to the required temperature must have been enormous. The most important place to have machicolations was over the gatehouse but in some castles they were built where they could be of no possible use. In later pseudo-castles, of the type which were built in the eighteenth or nineteenth century to give the owner a sense of importance, false machicolations were put in any place where they might be thought to impress. However, anyone who has studied medieval castles properly should not be deceived for a moment.

In the first two centuries of castle building in this country the architects were reluctant to allow anything but the narrowest of slits in the side walls – which were permitted in order to let in a little light and provide some ventilation. However, when bastion towers were introduced, the possibilities of these apertures as arrow slits were soon seen. Even so they were very sparingly used at first. Windows came in very slowly and they cannot have admitted much light for a long time for they were filled with iron grilles. The large windows you sometimes see in Norman keeps – such as at Kenilworth – were put in much later. In the early days it would have been suicidal to put in large windows: they would have admitted light and air but they would have let in the enemy, too.

On most of the towers you see on castles, and sometimes all along the base of the walls, you will notice that the masonry juts gently outwards. This is known by the misleading term of battering and the projection is usually known as a battered plinth. The object was not only to make the base of the walls more resistant to battering-rams and the like but also to provide a means of deflecting missiles dropped from above. The wielders of battering-rams protected themselves by metal coverings which were also fireproof. However, if you wished to inflict

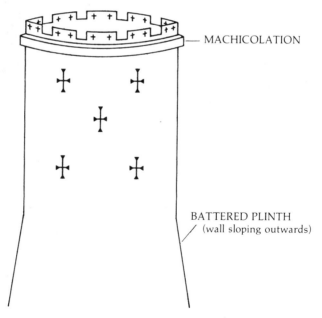

— MACHICOLATION

BATTERED PLINTH
(wall sloping outwards)

Fig. 5.

Fig 5: A tower in a thirteenth-century castle. Note the arrow loops which permitted both longbows and crossbows to be used. Around the top is a machicolation – a stone projection with a slotted floor through which missiles could be dropped.

casualties among the battering-ram party you bounced your red-hot iron bars off the battered plinth so that they landed among the people holding the battering-ram. There were other ways of checking a ram, such as lowering sacking pads to deaden the impact on the wall or gripping the end of the ram with a huge pair of tongs.

Castles built in the thirteenth and fourteenth centuries have a number of easily identifiable features. In the thirteenth century there was a lot of experimentation, not always successful. At one point it was decided that a castle built in the form of a circular tower would probably be invulnerable. Some such castles were effective, but some were too small and others did not have the bastion towers in the right position. However, during the thirteenth century a new type of castle was being developed. The older patterns all had a form of longitudinal defence; the attacker had to fight his way first through one bailey, then through a second, then to the keep. This certainly delayed him, but it meant that once he had captured one bailey he had an excellent base for further operations. Longitudinal castles continued to be built where the ground was particularly suitable for them, such as on a spur. If there was no suitable crag for a site, the builder merely selected a spur of land and cut a deep ditch to separate it from adjoining land. This effectively created a land island. Usually the sides of the spur – if it had been well chosen – were steep enough to deter a would-be attacker, but if it was thought that the defence needed further strengthening the whole area could be flooded to make a wide moat. This was done most effectively at Kenilworth, where two small streams were dammed to make a lake extending over 111 acres – and the castle therefore almost, but not quite, impregnable.

In any castle, whatever the period, a vulnerable point was the gateway and this, therefore, earned attention from all sides. Its vulnerability was obvious; it had to be opened and shut and therefore could not be as solid as the rest of the walls, and it had to be wide enough to permit the free passage of men and materials when the castle was at peace. The early gateways, as mentioned above, were on the first floor but they were too inconvenient for the complicated building which a castle later became. For a castle was not merely a means of attack and defence, it was an administrative headquarters, a legal centre, a military store, a centre of local government, and a home for a large number of people. Men were constantly going in and out of the main gate. A castle, it should never be forgotten, was a springboard. It controlled an area of about twenty-five miles radius. From it there would be constant patrols to see that no stranger had come into the district with ill intent. On the Welsh and Scottish borders this was particularly important.

So the gatehouse had to fulfil the normal functions of a doorway, but it also had to be defensible. This was achieved in various ways. One method was to protect it by building another defensive structure in front. This, known as the barbican, often formed another gatehouse ahead of the main one. The gatehouse proper was protected by a drawbridge which, when drawn up, acted as an additional line of defence. Behind the door itself – as sturdy as it could be made – there was probably a portcullis (an iron grille) which was let down from the roof. Often there would be more than one portcullis in the gatehouse passage. You can tell how many portcullises there were and where they were by looking for the grooves in the side walls into which they slotted. The gate was usually flanked by two towers of several storeys, one of which functioned as the guardroom. These flanking towers usually contained arrow slits which enabled flanking fire to be directed onto the unwelcome intruder from whichever direction he approached. Sometimes there were more than two towers; at Denbigh there are three, and a man who found himself in the middle of that complex would be in trouble indeed.

Some gatehouses were a form of miniature castle in themselves and could be defended front and rear. This curious development came in the thirteenth century when there were large numbers of mercenary troops in the country, mixed with English soldiers who had fought abroad; together they made a turbulent combination and were as likely as not to attack their own castellan (castle-holder) as the enemy. The castellan therefore felt the need to protect himself from any surge of indiscipline within the castle.

Additional points to look for in a gatehouse are *meurtrières* (literally, murder holes). They were openings in the walls or roof of the entrance passage through which intruders could be speared.

There may also be remains of internal gutters which seem unusual because they drain into the building rather than outside it. This was intentional, for they were not designed to carry away rainwater but to carry water to flood the lower gatehouse in the event of the enemy setting it on fire. Many attempts at putting out fires fail because the firemen cannot get to the heart of the conflagration. These gutters are the equivalent of the modern fire sprinkler.

In some castles it is possible to see the winding machinery for the portcullis, as in the Bloody Tower in the Tower of London. This is still in working order. Considerable ingenuity was required to make sure that a portcullis worked smoothly and efficiently. Its huge weight, combined with the small space available for the machinery, meant that an elaborate system of levers had to be used.

Staircases were designed with the same cunning as went into the remainder of the architecture. Capturing a castle was a battle of attrition. It was not sufficient merely to break through the gatehouse or scale the walls; every portion of the castle had to be taken. If it were not, a sudden counter-attack in the middle of the night could prove disastrous. But capturing the entire castle meant going up every staircase and into every room. Most staircases wind away to the right. That gave advantage to the defender retreating upwards: the attacker was at a disadvantage because when he tried to use his sword arm he was constantly banging it against the centre pillar. However, it was appreciated that there might be occasions – perhaps in a counter-attack – where the occupants wanted a stairway to their own advantage. Thus at Beaumaris you will find that six stairways turn left while only four turn right. At Caerphilly seven turn right and two left. In some castles the internal passageways were made so complicated that an attacker would constantly be frustrated. For example, it would be possible to ascend to the battlements, but just before one reached the gatehouse one would come to a dead end. Eventually these complex internal passages became even more of a nuisance to the defenders than they were to the attackers, and nowadays it is usually possible to move freely from one section to another without having to descend to ground level at intervals.

Another form of gateway not to be missed is the postern or sallyport. Today, with the actual gate usually missing, they may not look very impressive. Their function was twofold. If the defenders decided to abandon the castle altogether, the sallyport was a useful means of slipping away. It was usually situated at a point where the attackers would be unlikely – if not unable – to approach it, and it often came out onto a river where a few convenient boats were moored. But the sallyport had another important function. When a castle was attacked, the assault-party would bring up huge war engines, such as siege-towers and catapults. At night or in misty weather a party of defenders would often slip out by the sallyport and try to set fire to, or otherwise immobilise, these machines. In some sieges these forages from the sallyport by the defenders could be so disconcerting that the whole organisation of the siege was ruined. The drawback to sallyports was that they could sometimes be left open either by carelessness or treachery. Constantinople fell because a careless soldier left open a sallyport and a large party of attackers got in before they were discovered. The purpose of the sallyport was to turn defence into attack and exploit that great military asset, surprise. It was unfortunate if the tables were turned and the initiative and the sallyport fell to the attackers.

War engines were of various types, and were nearly as formidable as the firearms which eventually replaced them. They worked on the principal of bows or slings. The simplest form of bow, as we know, depends on bending a springy wood or metal frame. The greater the tension, the longer the range. The most powerful of the traditional bows were the longbows which could send an arrow several hundred yards and, at shorter distances, could be accurate enough to kill small animals. But a longbow required strength for its 70-pound pull. A longbowman could pick off opponents who unwisely exposed themselves on castle walls; he was as quick and deadly as a modern sniper. Slower, but more powerful, was the crossbow which created tension by winding or levering back the string. It launched a bolt or quarrel and had twice the range of the longbow, but was much slower to operate. Very large forms of crossbow were built and these hurled giant bolts which could split a door. They were called ballistas.

However, the most popular (with the users) were the weapons based on the sling principle. Even simple slings can be lethal, as the David and Goliath story shows, and it is interesting to think that a store of 20,000 slingstones was found at Maiden Castle – those that were *left* after the castle had been captured. Groups of men on the march were sometimes caught in an ambush by a shower of slingstones which would cause devastation from silent, unexpected and unseen attackers.

Larger slings were called 'mangonels'. They work on the same principle as a boy uses to make a ruler launch pellets. You tie two pieces of elastic between two solid objects then insert the ruler between them. Wind it up until the elastic is completely tense then put the missile on the end which, when the ruler is released, flies off at speed. Having no elastic our ancestors used hair; it was usually horse hair but human hair, plaited into a form of rope, was more tensile and thus better. Such a weapon could launch a quarter of a ton (or more) of rock at a wall. With practice considerable accuracy was achieved. On impact, the rock would splinter and kill like shrapnel. Variations in missiles were a dead horse (to spread disease) or a captured spy or a courier whose message had not found favour. These machines, twenty or thirty of which might be in action at the same time, were used not only by the besiegers but also by the besieged from inside the castle as a form of counter-attack.

Another variation was the trebuchet which worked on the counterpoise principle of having a great weight at one end of an arm on a fulcrum. The other end was pulled down, gradually raising the weight. Then the missile was loaded on and the weight was released. Gravity thus supplied the propulsion power.

Deadly weapons are often given affectionate nicknames such as Brown Bess (the musket), sweet lips (a Civil War cannon) and Big Bertha (a huge gun); mangonels, which were used by the Romans, were called onagers. An onager was a wild ass, but whether the name was used because the mangonel had a kick like a wild ass or because of the fact that it tilted over on firing, thus appearing to kick up its legs like a wild animal, is not known.

Fashions change in military matters as they do in everything else. Until the thirteenth century it had been assumed that the best design for a castle was longitudinal. However, as the result of experience in the Middle East during the Crusades, a number of fresh ideas came into Europe. One was the concentric pattern. This, as may be seen at Harlech and Beaumaris, was to build one castle inside another. The assailant would first of all be confronted with an outer wall and perhaps a moat, a short distance away from the main block. The outer wall

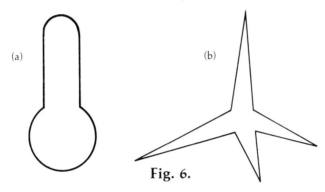

(a)

(b)

Fig. 6.

Fig 6: Defences:

  (a) *A gunport as used in fifteenth-century castles. The noise, smell and vibration caused by guns made them almost as much of a nuisance to the defender as to the attacker;*

  (b) *a caltrop (or caltrap). Whichever way the caltrop fell, one spike pointed upwards. They were used against men and horses, and are still used today against vehicles.*

would be studded with bastion towers and would be the first obstacle. It would not stop the attacker for long but it would effectively prevent him from making a surprise attack. Thus, when he came to the next point the whole garrison would be ready to receive him.

The first outer wall of the main block would be a much more formidable obstacle. It would be pierced with arrow loops of two types. The upright loops would be for longbows and they were ingeniously cut to give maximum protection to the man inside while at the same time enabling him to manoeuvre his bow and shoot at angles. The horizontal openings would be for crossbows, which had a longer range but a much slower discharge. As the attacker approached this wall he would receive a hail of arrows and would be none too comfortable underfoot for the ground would be covered with hundreds of caltrops. Caltrops were simple devices made of four spikes so designed that however they fell one spike would always be uppermost. They were particularly damaging to horses. Apart from the caltrops on the surface, the ground had probably been prepared with concealed pits, like elephant traps. The covering of these traps would easily bear the weight of two or three people but when a body of armed men or a piece of siege machinery went over it would collapse.

INTRODUCTION

In an attack on a castle the main attack would probably be at the gatehouse. Here, as elsewhere around the castle, the attacker would not only be fired on from the nearby wall but also from the taller walls of the inner castles, which could range over the top of the outer walls.

Every success would be dearly bought. If the attacker broke through the entrance he would find himself having to turn to the right on the stairs and thus be at a considerable disadvantage in using his sword arm. If his force broke completely through the outer wall and wished to take a battering-ram to the next he would find the captured space too narrow for the purpose and too small to contain all the men he needed for the next stage of the assault. Medieval tacticians were expert at luring an opponent to a place where he appeared to be successful but was actually in a position of great vulnerability.

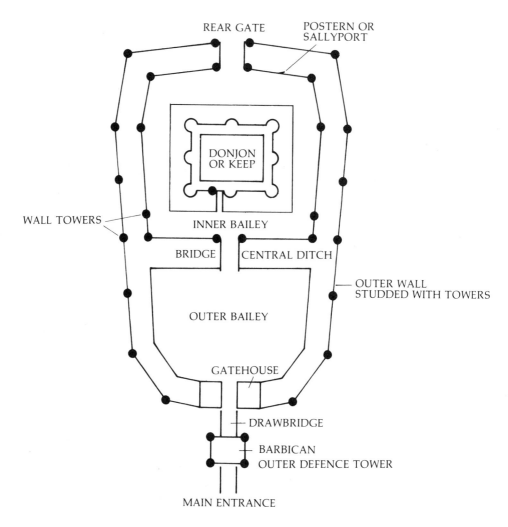

Fig. 7.

Fig 7: A linear castle, as at Conwy or Chepstow.

In the late fourteenth and early fifteenth centuries, castle builders concluded that many of these arrangements made internal movement too slow and frustrating. Although they still adhered to the principle of overlapping defences, flanking fire, and one point covering another, they decided that the advantage of interior lines had been lost. Interior lines means that the defender has less distance to cover than the attacker, and it is thus easier for him to bring all his defences to bear at the point where the attack is strongest. If, however, the interior is cluttered up with buildings, he will be unable to do this and his advantage is lost. In consequence, some of the castles of the fourteenth and fifteenth centuries, like Bodiam and Herstmonceux, left the interior as clear as possible.

Early castles had been built of flint and rubble. This combination does not sound very substantial, but when bonded together by medieval cement was remarkably tough. At Caerphilly and Bridgnorth you may see towers which have been leaning at a dangerous angle ever since an attempt was made to blow them up hundreds of years ago. There are others like them. Most of the early castles had their rough flint covered with ashlar. Ashlar is the name given to rectangular blocks of stone used for facing. Much of this facing was later prised off by local people for building use near by, but plenty remains. Of course, castles vary in different parts of the country according to the building materials available.

In the fifteenth century, some castles were built of brick. There is a very interesting and unusual one at Tattershall in Lincolnshire; it is in the form of a tall tower, though once it also had extensive additional buildings. There is a brick castle at Shirburn in Oxfordshire, although unfortunately at the time of writing it is not open to the public. There is another at Caister, Norfolk, and another at Kirby Muxloe, near Leicester.

By the late fifteenth century most castles had become reasonably comfortable as residences. It is, of course, doubtful whether the old stone castles were as dank and uncomfortable as they seem today for there would have been fires day and night in the huge fireplaces for most of the year and our ancestors loved bright colours. The White Tower in London was painted white; and other castles were also painted in dazzling colours which have long since been washed away. Around the walls of a castle in peacetime there would be herb gardens, and their products, particularly lavender, would be left in bowls at frequent intervals in order to sweeten the air in the rooms. Later, tapestries would be hung on the walls. As we know that many medieval monarchs and noblemen were tremendous dandies, who wore every absurdity of fashion from head to foot, it is not likely that they managed without silken bed coverings and other luxuries.

A remarkable thing about medieval life was the way that food was prepared. All you are likely to see today in the kitchens is a fairly crude form of oven. This would be adequate for baking bread or roasting a joint, but to see how the rest of the meal was cooked we have to use our imagination. We know that the cooks coloured the food bright red, bright green, bright yellow or black, and we know that they made very complicated pies. Many foods were reduced to a paste, then reshaped; all were highly spiced. But we shall have to trust to our imagination in the kitchen if we are to visualise the preparation of swans, ducks, hares, linnets, thrushes, deer, salmon, trout, eels, herrings, and the dozens of other foods which were eaten on festive occasions.

The other important part of castle life which it is difficult to comprehend today is recreation. There was, of course, a lot of work to fill up the day but not everyone

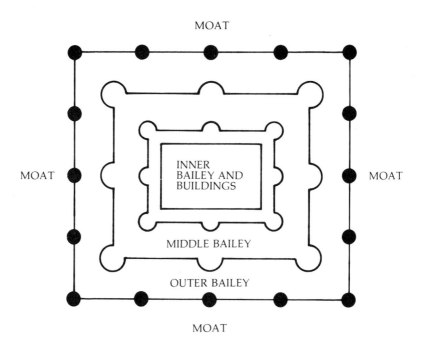

MOAT

MOAT

INNER BAILEY AND BUILDINGS

MOAT

MIDDLE BAILEY

OUTER BAILEY

MOAT

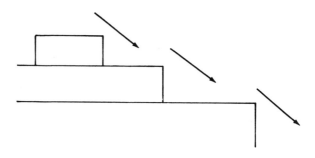

Fig. 8.

Fig 8: A concentric castle, as at Harlech or Beaumaris. The inner buildings and towers were taller than the outer ones, thereby enabling the defenders to concentrate their fire on an attacker.

had to do it. Drinking, talking and gambling took up time indoors, but outside time was largely passed in practising warlike occupations. In the area round the castle there would be a space like a football pitch set aside for training. It might include a tilt-yard where minor tournaments were held, but it usually contained enough flat ground in which to execute manoeuvres and practise sword-play. Horsemanship was also of vital importance, but, as often as possible, men engaged in the chase, and that is outside our scope here.

By the end of the fifteenth century, siege warfare involving castles had fallen into decline and differences of political opinion were settled on the open battlefield, as at Bosworth. Many people therefore found it more convenient to live in a building that resembled a modern house more than a castle: thus the manor-house came into fashion. Many manor-houses had been in existence for centuries, but not everybody had the confidence to live in one although most were moated and defensible against minor attacks. Of these, more later. But there was still a need for fortresses, many of them on the coast for times of danger. During his reign, Henry VII somewhat rashly managed to offend a number of potentially formidable opponents at the same time. It seemed that, in spite of his navy, there was an excellent chance that he might be invaded by France. Later in 1545, French troops did succeed in landing on the Isle of Wight, but the damage they were able to do was limited. The fact that England was now in danger of full-scale invasion caused a swift appraisal of existing defences as well as planning for new ones. Many old castles, particularly those in coastal areas, were repaired and strengthened. It was now realised that their defensive potential, even in the days of artillery, was considerable. It also appeared as though some of the dramatic successes of artillery in the previous hundred years had been due more to the crumbling of morale than of masonry. The efficiency of medieval masonry against gunfire would be proved during the next century when at the height of the Civil War many old castles, notably Corfe, in Dorset, proved quite unbreachable by the latest seventeenth-century artillery. In World War II, many other castles in different parts of the world proved that medieval masonry had effective resistance to military fire-power. They did not, of course, last very long, but they lasted much longer than anyone would have ventured to predict.

Henry VIII, deeply conscious of the possibility of a full-scale invasion on the south coast, decided to build a series of forts which would combine the best features of the old with the best of the new. These were to be artillery forts, designed to offer considerable resistance to enemy gunfire but at the same time to carry considerable firepower of their own. As the visitor to Walmer, Deal, Camber, St Mawes, or Pendennis will immediately notice, they carried on the principle of the concentric castle while at the same time offering the maximum number of deflecting surfaces. Deal looks like a series of flat drums piled one upon another, first six at the base, then four, then one crowning the top. However, the design of different castles varied somewhat in the details. Possibly the most interesting to the visitor is Walmer, for it had the added importance of being the residence of the Warden of the Cinque Ports. Walmer has magnificent gardens and many relics of the Duke of Wellington, victor of Waterloo. Most of the original guns are still in position in these castles and it will be noted that there are numerous loopholes from which supporting artillery could fire with advantage. The defensive asset of a broad ditch was also incorporated. As many of these castles – particularly the earlier ones – were at important strategic points, it is not surprising that they were refurbished for use at subsequent times of national peril. When Napoleon threatened to cross the Channel during the Napoleonic Wars, these coastal defences were made ready to receive him, and when Hitler offered the same threat in the 1940s another programme of modernisation was put into effect. Henry VIII's castles were particularly suitable for use by the British Army in 1940, and today the visitor will find clear indication of which parts of the masonry belong to 1540 and which to 1940. Even more striking and deceptive are the adaptations made to the Roman–Norman forts at Pevensey and Portchester.

Later residential castles

The residential castles are, broadly speaking, of three types. There is the defensible manor-house, such as Stokesay in Shropshire; there is the medieval castle, which was subsequently made comfortable and thus habitable; and there is the house built in the form of a castle for reasons of prestige rather than defence. A good example of the first is Stokesay – no longer inhabited. The second category includes palaces such as Windsor, Balmoral and Falkland, and also castles such as Inverary, Berkeley and Broughton, which are open to the public at certain times but are also the homes of their owners. The third category includes castles which were rebuilt, usually on the site of a medieval stronghold which was demolished. Typical of such castles are Castell Coch, near Cardiff, a replica thirteenth-century castle, and Belvoir, Leicestershire, which was rebuilt in 1800. However, castles do not fall easily into categories, for their owners tinkered with them century after century and a well-kept castle today may include specimens of every period of building. Thus Warwick, a castle which no one should miss seeing, includes the original motte, the famous medieval Beauchamp towers, and a collection of magnificent buildings dating from the seventeenth century.

Today castles seem quiet and peaceful. In their heyday they were neither. They were immensely busy, lively places, in peace or war. They were full of fighting men, cooks, woodcutters, smiths, armourers, butchers, builders, women and children and a host of others. There was undoubtedly a lot of flirtation, a lot of roguery, and a lot of laughter in castles. With a little imaginative effort it is possible to visualise them all again.

Haunted castles

Many castles have strange stories and legends attached to them. Most people have an open mind about the existence of ghosts, although suspecting that imagination and optical illusion account for a lot of supposed sightings. This is clearly a subject for which rational explanations do not come easily, and seeing ghosts may be a recognised ability that some, but not all, people possess, as some practise water-divining or extrasensory perception. It is interesting to reflect that if a medieval castle-dweller had forecast television, or radio, electricity or the telephone, he would have been locked up (perhaps burnt) as a dangerous lunatic and heretic; certainly no one would have believed such fantastic delusions!

There are many varieties of ghost; some are friendly but some sinister, unpleasant and perhaps evil. Ghost-hunting in ruined castles can be dangerous physically, for it is all too easy in the dark to stumble and break a limb. There are worse experiences in ghost-hunting than actually seeing a ghost.

As this book is a guide to material places and buildings, the subject of alleged hauntings is treated separately on a believe-it-or-not basis. Undoubtedly most ghost stories can be dismissed as pure fantasy but there are a few which come from reliable sources, sometimes confirmed by others, which are not easily explained. The writer recalls being told by someone who once lived in the Chapel Cloisters at Windsor Castle (where clergy of St George's Chapel live) that one night he was awakened by a great clatter in the central passage through the cloisters. He and his wife looked out of their bedroom window and saw what they assumed to be a noisy rehearsal for a nocturnal Elizabethan pageant, in fact a disorderly procession. It passed through and the sounds died away. But it had not been a pageant and there was no explanation. It was not seen again nor had it been known to have occurred before.

There is another reputed ghost in the Horseshoe Cloisters and a more sinister one on the terrace which has several times been seen by sentries who challenge it and find the experience very uncanny. Queen Elizabeth I is said to haunt the library and George III the rooms in which he spent his last, insane days, plucking at a harp. There is also a highly improbable legend about Herne the Hunter in Windsor Great Park.

The Tower of London, as might be expected, has a chilling company of ghosts. The long history of executions and even murders within its walls and of notable prisoners who were executed outside includes those of Anne Boleyn, Sir Walter Raleigh, the boy princes, Lady Jane Grey, Henry VI, the Duke of Clarence, Guy Fawkes, Lord Lovat, and many lesser figures, including spies. An unpleasant aspect of the ghosts in the Tower is that they are not so often seen as experienced. Sceptical and rational people who have walked around the Tower at night have confessed to feeling distinctly unnerved, perhaps threatened, on occasions, in certain parts. Anne Boleyn is a harmless ghost who has been seen many times – as she has also at Hever Castle, which was her home. She is said to appear, as are many others, in the Chapel of St Peter ad Vincula, which was the last resting place of many headless corpses. But it is not the helpless victims of the Tower, Anne Boleyn, pathetic Lady Jane Grey, poor mad Henry VI, or foolish Clarence, who arouse fear but the evil spirits of their murderers, the torturers, the men who would find no deed too evil for them to perform; they are even less likely to be resting easily in their graves.

A royal ghost whom one might expect to see is Edward II who was murdered at Berkeley Castle but he has never appeared; however, that of his favourite, Piers de Gaveston, is reputed to appear at Scarborough, and that of his wife Isabella, who helped plot his death, at Castle Rising where she ended her days. Isabella's screams are also said to be heard at Nottingham Castle where her murderous husband was arrested and taken from her.

Warwick Castle is haunted by Sir Fulke Greville who was stabbed by a servant; Herstmonceux by a phantom drummer who does not appear, and Dover by one who does, though without a head. Phantom drumming is attributed to a number of Scottish castles where it is invariably considered to be a warning of evil in store.

Arundel has the ghost of a man in blue who seems to be looking for something in a book in the library but there is no story to account for it. Rochester has several ghosts but the most surprising is that of Charles Dickens, who wished to be buried there instead of in Westminster Abbey! Ludlow claims the ghost of Marion de la Bruyère who betrayed the castle to her lover and then killed herself in remorse. The story is well documented but the ghost is less convincing.

Scotland has an impressive tally of ghosts, some being linked to clan feuds when appalling atrocities were committed. The massacre of Glencoe was by no means unique. Of the Scottish castles, Glamis probably has the most numerous collection of ghosts and Castle Urquhart on Loch Ness the most bizarre. Urquhart is alleged to be haunted by a soldier and an evil spirit connected with the supposed monster

INTRODUCTION

(it has been exorcized). Sinister ghosts are to be found at Hermitage, at Rosslyn, at Inverary and at Edzell.

In Wales, Caerphilly has a woman spectre, St David's in Glamorgan various ill-omened ladies, and Powis a ghost from the distant past.

This is merely a selection of the most famous. Ghosts do not seem to appear at any particular time, nor necessarily to people who expect to see them. They tend to disappear for centuries then emerge again. There are, however, very few ghosts of the distant past. Some of the oldest appeared in York to a policeman. He saw a Roman patrol returning to the city, looking tired and dishevelled, and walking straight through a wall. But York is full of ghosts.

Few ghosts materialise when investigated scientifically but ghosts *have* been photographed and uncanny sounds have been recorded. People who don't believe in ghosts are much less likely to see one than those who do, but it does not always happen that way.

People who live in haunted castles do not always welcome inquiries about ghosts and often deny all knowledge of them. They have learned to live with their ghosts and not to offend them. At breakfast one member of the family may say '– was about last night'. 'Yes,' will be the reply, 'I heard it too.' But there the matter ends – until it walks again.

Some castles and their reputed ghosts

Astley:	The Duke of Suffolk, father of Lady Jane Grey.
Blackness:	General Dalyell, founder of the Scots Greys (now Royal Scots Dragoon Guards).
Caerphilly:	A spectral woman whose appearance was a sign of coming death or disaster.
Carlisle:	A woman; a large dog.
Dunraven:	A green lady.
Dunstanburgh:	The Earl of Lancaster, executed for treason in 1322.
Dunster:	A skeleton.
Glamis:	The monster; a grey lady; a man with a long beard; mysterious knockings; the woman with a bundle in her arms; the white lady.
Hadleigh:	A wraith.
Hermitage:	Mary, Queen of Scots; Lord de Soulis.
Hever:	Anne Boleyn.
Inverary:	A galley in the lake; a phantom harper; ravens.
Lancaster:	Various unknown figures.
Lowther:	A coach and horses.
Ludlow:	Marion de la Bruyère.
Nottingham:	Queen Isabella.
Tower of London:	See above text.
Warwick:	Sir Fulke Greville; a large dog.
Windsor:	See above text.

Tracing your ancestors

As mentioned earlier, some of your ancestors must have lived in a castle somewhere, at some time. But whether they commanded it or merely helped with the cooking will be difficult to find out. However, tracing your family back – on both sides – is a fascinating activity from which you will learn a lot about history, a lot of geography, and a lot about yourself. Many people start on tracing their ancestors with all sorts of optimistic fantasies, such as finding a millionaire uncle who does not know where to leave his money, or discovering aristocratic relations, preferably rich. Such hopes may be disappointed, but the searchers are likely to find their efforts rewarded in other ways.

Having written down everything anyone in your family knows, the next step is to go to the places where the oldest members of the family lived and visit the local church. There may be headstones in the churchyard or in the church itself and there might be parish registers which, with the permission of the vicar, you may be able to study – however, many parish registers have now been transferred to County Record Offices. There is also a large collection of parish registers at the Society of Genealogists, 37 Harrington Gardens, London, SW7. You may inspect the records there for a small fee, but you would find membership of the Society a great help. When you find a piece of information, record all the details available, especially full names and dates of birth and death. If the dates are not complete you need not despair, but if they are you will find them useful to distinguish one member of a family from another when the same Christian names appear frequently. Some families might have a tree like this:

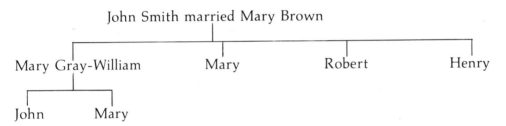

Here there are two John Smiths and three Mary Smiths all living at the same time. In these cases, dates are most valuable.

Another useful source is: The General Register Office, St Catherine's House, 10 Kingsway, London, WC2. Here the records of all births, marriages and deaths since 1837 are kept and are available for inspection. The Scots have their offices at New Register House, Edinburgh.

The Public Record Office, Portugal Street, London, WC2, has the census records since 1841 and these give the names, ages and occupations of everyone in the households. This is where it is important to know where your ancestors lived. The Public Record Office also holds military and naval records and criminal records. The latter include the names of criminals transported to Australia but it may or may not be a comfort to know that many of the crimes were very minor ones, by today's standards. It was once possible to be hanged for stealing a handkerchief, or a chicken, or for carving one's initials on Westminster Bridge. Unfortunately very few Parish Records were kept before the early 1600s and even those that were are incomplete, as are some later ones. Reading an early register which has not been transcribed is not easy but to encounter items like 'Buried a pauper. Name unknown' is like looking through a window into another, harsher world.

Other sources are old wills at Somerset House, Strand, London, WC2 (which may be visited) and old Post Office directories (available through libraries).

However law-abiding you may be, there is a good chance that your family appeared in the courts at some time in its history and this will be on record in lists of fines.

By the time you have gone back to the seventeenth century you will have a good idea of the places in which many of your ancestors lived and the names of the other families with which you are connected. If you assume that on average, there is a new generation every twenty-five years this gives four to a century. Starting with two parents in 1980, and proceeding arithmetically backwards, you will have four grandparents, eight great-grandparents, thirty-two great-great-grandparents who cover approximately the most recent hundred years. Using the same method, and this time starting with the thirty-two, you will find that you had approximately five hundred ancestors a hundred years earlier.

After two more centuries of the same process you find that the number of your ancestors has become something like 64,000. Take it back another two centuries and your ancestors number eight million, which is more than the population of the country, so obviously you are related to some several times over but to others not at all. This vast collection of ancestors will not be spread evenly but will tend to group around certain areas – areas where a castle was probably the central point. A good proportion of your ancestors may have been natural children through love, rape, or other reasons. However, it was not always as simple as it may seem. If the comely wife of the gamekeeper bore a child bearing a close resemblance to the lord of the manor, her ladyship might well bear a child who looked remarkably like the handsome captain of the archers.

If one of your ancestors seems to have had a coat of arms – and there were hundreds of them – you may find it a help in tracing your family. The coat of arms originated in a design on a shield so that a man in armour could be recognised on the battlefield. Originally they were very simple; later they became very complicated. However a man was not automatically entitled to bear his father's arms: his own coat was 'differenced' by some minor change. Sometimes a knight who had fallen out of favour, perhaps through rebelling or failing to obey a royal command, would quietly abandon his arms and try to live in obscurity. In later years attempts were made to trace all the people entitled to bear arms so as to tax them, and this led to the County Visitation in the seventeenth century. The results of the visitation were printed in the Harleian Manuscripts and they are a useful, though disconnected, source of pedigrees. For more information on heraldry, it is best to read a reliable book on the subject such as Sir Iain Moncrieffe's very witty and well illustrated *Simple Heraldry*, or if you are really serious about that coat of arms consult The College of Arms, Queen Victoria Street, London, EC4. Proving your right to a coat of arms can be an expensive undertaking.

Living in castles
Visitors to castles often look around the ancient walls and wonder what daily life was like in medieval times. What time did people get up, go to bed; how did they amuse themselves; who organised it all? There is no doubt that in a castle in which two or three hundred people lived and were employed there must have been considerable organisation. Exceptional administrative foresight was required in a castle which in peacetime held a very small garrison, perhaps thirty, but on the approach of danger would house three hundred.

When Henry III besieged Bedford Castle in 1220, fifteen thousand crossbow bolts were sent from Corfe Castle in Dorset; charcoal came from Gloucester, and knights came from Lancaster. When he besieged Kenilworth in 1265, assault barges, to cross the wide lake, were brought from Chester. At this time castles had been part of English life for some two hundred years, and would remain so for another two hundred at least. After that people lived in more comfortable residences.

When considering life in castles we are therefore looking at a span of some four hundred years in which life did not stand still. When William II lived in the Tower of London in the 1090s a lot of wine was drunk, hair was worn very long, his favourite companions were homosexuals and harlots, clothes were fantastic to the point of absurdity (shoes had such long points to them that they had to be tied by strings to the waist if the wearer was to walk at all), and sometimes the court stayed up all night and slept all day. All the same, when the occasion demanded they all turned out in armour and fought like demons on the battlefield.

Greater comfort and certain refinements of debauchery came in after the Crusades. Food was more varied, carpets or tapestries appeared, lavatories were built into the walls, and there was a complex arrangement of servants – botilers or butlers (who saw to the serving or storing of the wine), cooks, bakers, chandlers (for candles), blacksmiths, grooms, stewards. Food was dried or otherwise preserved for the winter. Bread (pan) was kept in the pantry; lard from the ubiquitous pig, in the larder. The outside staff of millers and tillers and ploughmen and butchers was even larger. Bowyers made bows, fletchers made arrows for them. Cooper and hooper made casks. Archers practised with bowmen; fuller cleaned cloth and dyer dyed it. Salter controlled salt; souter mended shoes. Porter watched the comings and goings. Further afield were hunters, hawkers, falconers and fishers. Women could do most of these tasks as well as men but pretended not to be able to; they also dressed hair, made clothes, tended the sick, and stirred up trouble. Quarrels began because men were showing off to women and competing for their favours or had had a row with one. It all kept the blood moving.

Much of the time food was frugal, but on special occasions like Christmas, weddings, feast days, or the arrival of a distinguished visitor the extravagance and waste were astonishing. Chickens, hares, rabbits, geese, partridges, pigs, eels, swans, peacocks, salmon, trout were served – all eaten with the fingers (the fork had not been invented) but to an elaborate ritual of hand-washing. Wine was drunk in large quantities because it would not keep; ale was served liberally because it was easily brewed. Books on etiquette enjoined men to keep their hands and knives clean, to take moderate portions, and to keep their hands out of the clothes of the lady sitting next to them.

Women had few legal or official rights but exercised considerable power by other means. Some, like Isabel de Warenne in the twelfth century, were left vast fortunes; she had estates in twelve counties. Noble women were married young, perhaps at the age of five, as a matter of economics and politics. Women of this class were enthusiasts for hunting and allied sports. Castle management was left to stewards and chancellors, many of whom lined their own pockets and, if undetected, became minor lordlings as a result. Less wealthy wives became expert household managers, keeping the keys of the stores in their own charge, seeing that tasks were properly completed, and even commanding the garrison if the castle was attacked while the husband was away. In addition a woman found time for music, for elaborate hair styles and dresses, for bearing children (two or three by the time she was twenty; some women were grandmothers by the age of thirty), and was by no means inhibited, though discreet, in matters of sex. Children had a very short childhood; if boys, they were on a horse almost as soon as they could walk and often on the battlefield at the age of twelve as pages. Girls were given no special favours, though they might be betrothed. Often children of both sexes were sent to another household for upbringing and some rudimentary education; it was one way of ensuring that they were not spoilt!

The lady of the house supervised the herb garden which produced flavourings for food and remedies to be put in the medicine chest. The latter included various cordials and cures. The basis for most of them was what we would now call weeds: chickweed made poultices for abscesses; clover tea relieved bronchitis and whooping cough; daisies made an ointment for bruises and wounds; nettles were for anaemia, and groundsel made a balm for chapped hands. There were dozens more of these natural remedies and the chatelaine knew them all.

There were numerous fireplaces and fuel was unlimited, so castles were warm, noisy, living places with much coming and going. Life tended to be short and precarious so there was much sense in enjoying it and festivals like Christmas, Easter, Michaelmas, Shrove Tuesday, Candlemas, and May Day. On May Day everyone went into the woods to gather flowers and greenery. People of all ages and kinds, even the priests, joined in and some got lost and spent the night in the forest. People shed their usual characters on other days too, like Whitsun and Midsummer Eve, but Easter was the first and least restrained of the summer holidays. It was like the Fasching Carnival Week in Munich, and all very different from May Day today with its dreary political processions or parades of tanks and guns.

There was less material but more spiritual comfort than today. You believed in God even if you did laugh at the priest sometimes; you worked hard and frequently had less food than you would have liked. But every so often for one reason or another the restraints were lifted and you let yourself go. Afterwards you could hardly believe what you remembered doing – but you looked forward to the next time even more.

The Evolution of Castles and Forts in Britain

3000 BC	Stone Age. Hilltop camps for cattle. Constructed with stone or bone tools.
2000 BC	Bronze Age. More hilltop forts.
900–100 BC	Iron Age forts. Two thousand approximately. Often extensions of previous forts. Tribal or anti-invasion strongholds.
55 and 54 BC	Julius Caesar invades Britain with reconnaissance forces.
AD 43	Roman invasion and occupation of Britain. Roads, camps, forts (Pevensey, Portchester).
447	Romans leave Britain. Saxons already coming in.
500–1000	Saxon, Angles and Danes invade. Towns fortified by earthworks.
1066	Norman invasion. Motte and bailey (mound and enclosure) castles surrounded by deep ditches.
11th century	Mostly wooden buildings but some stone, e.g. Tower of London. Many border castles near Wales.
12th century	Anarchy. Stephen – Matilda wars. Many motte and bailey castles built but soon abandoned and demolished.

13th century	More sophisticated castles incorporating ideas from the Middle East brought back by Crusaders.
1346–1430	Hundred Years War with France.
14th century	Sophisticated concentric castles. Walled towns.
15th century	Return to simpler design and brickwork castles. More comfort. Development of manor houses.
16th century	Henry VIII. Shore castles for gun mounting.
17th century	Former castles put to use in Civil War 1642–1651.
18th century	Development of country mansions, sometimes called 'castles' but not defensible.
19th century	Many shore forts (Martello towers etc) in Napoleonic Wars. Fear of French invasion led to forts around south coast.
20th century	Shore forts, pill-boxes etc.

ENGLAND

1 AVON
2 BERKSHIRE
3 CAMBRIDGESHIRE
4 CHESHIRE
5 CORNWALL
6 CUMBRIA
7 DERBYSHIRE
8 DEVONSHIRE
9 DORSET
10 DURHAM
11 ESSEX
12 GLOUCESTERSHIRE
13 HAMPSHIRE
14 HEREFORD
 AND WORCESTER
15 HERTFORDSHIRE
16 HUMBERSIDE
17 ISLE OF WIGHT
18 KENT
19 LANCASHIRE
20 LEICESTERSHIRE
21 LINCOLNSHIRE
22 LONDON
23 NORFOLK
24 NORTHAMPTONSHIRE
25 NORTHUMBERLAND
26 NOTTINGHAMSHIRE
27 OXFORDSHIRE
28 SHROPSHIRE
29 SOMERSET
30 STAFFORDSHIRE
31 SUFFOLK
32 SURREY
33 SUSSEX
34 TYNE AND WEAR
35 WARWICKSHIRE
36 WEST MIDLANDS
37 WILTSHIRE
38 YORKSHIRE

Because of its proximity to the Continent, south-east England needed many castles to guard potential invasion routes. Many of the sites had been chosen for a different purpose, that of conquering and holding down the country when William I invaded in 1066, but the tactical excellence of the sites made them equally valuable for protection against further intruders. A visitor could therefore well begin his tour of castles in this region (but it should not end there); he can see the Norman castles in the old Roman shore forts at Pevensey and Portchester, move on to Hastings and while there travel a few miles inland to see the site of the battle in the appropriately named town of Battle; here is marked the spot where Harold is said to have been killed and where William I founded a great abbey to commemorate his victory. Dover should be visited. The Romans were here too and left many traces. The great medieval castle has been in almost continuous military use, up to and including World War II. It often came under fire when this battered area of England was nicknamed 'Hellfire Corner'. Near Dover are Deal and Walmer, which were built to withstand the early cannon. The coast abounds with reminders of past dangers; there are the stubby little forts built by Pitt to counter the threat of Napoleonic invasion and there are concrete blockhouses, trench systems and rotting sandbags to recall the time when Hitler assembled his armada of boats across the Channel and the Luftwaffe fought with the Spitfires in the sky above.

Further inland he will come to Bodiam (Sussex) and Leeds (Kent), two of the most beautiful castles in the world. Bodiam was built to counter the threat from France in the Middle Ages: Leeds has a long history and was used as an emergency hospital in World War II.

From London the visitor will easily be able to visit both the Tower of London and Windsor Castle but both visits may take much longer than is expected as there is much to see and often many visitors to see it.

From the south-east to the south-west and the visitor will be in tranquil countryside. Sherborne, Farleigh Hungerford, Nunney and Dunster, in particular, will claim attention.

In the Midlands he will find Kenilworth in impressive ruin from which its great history may easily be visualised, and at Warwick and Rockingham magnificent and well-preserved castles which seem little changed from the day they were built centuries ago.

In the north the settings will be more stark and compelling. No impression of castles is complete unless you have seen Skipton, Helmsley, Scarborough, Pickering, York, Richmond, Alnwick and Norham.

BERKSHIRE

Berkshire has a variety of scenes to fascinate the traveller. It has the royal palace of Windsor, the ruined castle of Donnington, the Civil War battlefields of Newbury, some of the most beautiful reaches of the Thames, and the Downs with the mysterious, 3,000-year-old Berkshire Ridgeway crossing them. The Icknield Way, which is even older than the Ridgeway, in places runs close to it. The country is steeped in history: Alfred the Great defeated the Danes here, someone at some time carved the White Horse on the hillside, Reading and Newbury both had powerful castles, but both have since been completely demolished. Wallingford has tenth-century earthworks and a few traces (on private land) of what was once one of the most powerful castles in England. The remains may be seen from the road which leaves the town on the north side, but there is little to see.

DONNINGTON

The outstanding feature of Donnington today is the presence of the two huge drum-towers. Originally there were four, for this was a fourteenth-century rectangular castle. It had an interesting early history, and in 1415 it was owned by Thomas Chaucer, son of Geoffrey Chaucer the poet. Thence it passed by marriage to William de la Pole, Earl of Suffolk, who was murdered on the beach at Dover by persons unknown. At the start of the Civil War it was seized and garrisoned by Charles I. Traces of earthworks from this period may be seen. The castle withstood a heavy siege and was in the centre of the Second Battle of Newbury in 1644, after which, the garrison was allowed to surrender with the honours of war, i.e. to march out with drums beating and flags flying.

The castle is 1½ miles north-west of Newbury between the B4000 to Lambourn and the B4494 to Wantage. Do not take the new motorway.
Opening times are:
15 March–15 October, 9.30 a.m.–6.30 p.m. daily including Sunday;
16 October–14 March, 9.30 a.m.–4 p.m.
Closed Maundy Thursday, Good Friday, 24, 25, 26 December, 1 January.
The above are the normal Department of the Environment opening times.

Donnington

WINDSOR

Windsor Castle is a royal palace and has been described at the largest inhabited castle in the world. (A palace is the residence of a sovereign, an archbishop or bishop.) There is no point in trying to see Windsor quickly, for it only means that much of interest will be missed. Apart from the castle, there is Windsor itself, the Great Park and the Long Walk and nearby Eton College. Windsor is too large a subject to be covered in a book of this size and scope, but if you do not have all the time you need to see castles, you should try at least to see Windsor, Warwick, the White Tower (Tower of London), Edinburgh and Caernarfon. Comprehensive guide books are available in all of them, or you may join a guided party. This will ensure that you go around slowly enough to appreciate all the pictures, furniture, china, and relics.

Windsor is 21 miles west of London and the castle is in the centre of the town. The castle precincts are open normally from 10 a.m. to sunset. St George's Chapel is open 11 a.m.–3.45 p.m. on weekdays and 2.30–4 p.m. on Sundays. It is closed in January. The state apartments are normally open 10.30 a.m.–5 p.m. in the summer and 10.30 a.m.–3 p.m. in the winter (November to February). However, they are closed when Her Majesty the Queen is in residence, which is normally for six weeks at Easter, three weeks in June and three weeks at Christmas.

Windsor

CAMBRIDGESHIRE

Cambridgeshire swallowed up the old county of Huntingdonshire in the county boundary changes of 1974. Both counties had a number of small castles which have now completely vanished. The colleges of Cambridge University, which are open to visitors (and usually full of them) have much to teach the student of castle life. The dining-halls, with a High Table and wooden tables and benches in the main hall, are medieval in pattern. Often they have a minstrels' gallery, though it is unlikely to be used as such. The chapels, with intricate and beautiful stained-glass windows, are of the type which medieval castles possessed. Many of the colleges are built around a central court, as later castles were. Bear in mind that the architects who built colleges and cathedrals also built castles: unfortunately, many castles have fallen into ruin and what was once a superb building has now, all too often, become dilapidated, beyond recall.

CAMBRIDGE CASTLE

The castle, built originally by William the Conqueror, is now merely a grassy mound some 40 feet high, but it is worth a visit. In its heyday it saw plenty of fighting but lost all its masonry in the nineteenth century. The choice of site is impressive and shows the Norman skill in this strategic art. Even today you can see Leicester from the summit.

On the north side of the town near the river. Open at all times.

KIMBOLTON

The original castle here was the seat of the notorious Mandevilles but extensive rebuilding took place in the seventeenth and eighteenth centuries. In the latter period it was redesigned by Vanbrugh in classical style. Note the painted walls and ceilings.

8 miles north-west of St Neots on the A45 and 14 miles north of Bedford. Open Easter Sunday and Monday, Spring Bank Holiday Sunday and Monday, August Bank Holiday Monday, and 13 July to 31 August Sundays 2–6 p.m.

CHESHIRE

Cheshire has a fine military record, as it needed to have if it was to survive on the frontier of Wales. Cheshire-men made outstanding archers; the unexpected victory at Flodden in 1513 was partly due to their skill. Once there were many strong castles in Cheshire but most have now disappeared. Although Cheshire once had a strong castle, little of it now remains. However, some idea of the military strength of Chester may be gained by walking along the fourteenth-century ramparts of the old walls. Chester is a fascinating and beautiful town which has successfully resisted many enemies, including modern planning vandals and developers.

BEESTON

The castle bailey encloses a huge area, but much of this is overgrown with scrub. Clearance is being tackled but it may be some years before it is completed. However, the castle is very interesting to visit, even though getting from one part to another requires considerable physical exertion. Unlike many other castles, Beeston was never a residence but primarily a military strongpoint; as you stand at the summit of a 500 feet cliff, surrounded by the remains of very sturdy masonry, you may wonder how it could ever have been captured.

The first castle was built by Ranulf, Earl of Chester, in the early thirteenth century; the Chesters were a particularly warlike and volatile family. Beeston became a royal property but was occupied by Simon de Montfort between the Battle of Lewes (1264) and the Battle of Evesham (1265). Richard II is said to have buried his treasure here shortly before he was captured and murdered by his cousin who became Henry IV. The treasure has never been found and, looking over the area where it might lie, this fact is easy to understand.

In the Civil War Beeston was captured by eight Royalists who climbed the north wall, incredible though this feat may seem; the garrison of eighty surrendered, but the commander was later shot by his own men for cowardly incompetence. The castle was held by the Royalists for two years, but on its eventual fall was thoroughly slighted by the Roundheads.

A feature of the castle is the well – 370 feet deep!

Approximately half-way between Crewe and Chester on the A49 is Beeston village and castle. Department of the Environment opening times are now:
15 March–15 October, 9.30 a.m.–6.30 p.m. daily including Sunday;
16 October–14 March, 9.30 a.m.–4 p.m.
Closed Maundy Thursday, Good Friday, 24, 25, 26 December and 1 January.

CORNWALL

Cornwall is renowned for its tough fighting soldiers and sailors, for its tin and lead mines, for the dubious activities of wreckers on its dangerous coasts, for ghosts, and for delicious clotted cream. It is also rich with legends about King Arthur, who may well have been a Briton chief who used the county as a base when fighting campaigns against the Saxon invaders. Cornwall's scenery, variety and history make it a somewhat crowded holiday resort in high summer.

LAUNCESTON

The first castle was built by Robert of Mortain in the eleventh century on a hill which was shaped and made more dominant by the addition of an artificial motte. Originally, there was a wooden castle here, but later it was replaced by a shell-keep which spread the weight of the stonework over a wider area. There was once a large outer bailey here; much of it has disappeared but the remainder has been made into gardens.

In the fourteenth century Launceston was owned by the Black Prince. In the Civil War it was occupied by Royalists, but by the time it surrendered in 1646 was so damaged that it needed no further dismantling. In the second half of the seventeenth century George Fox, founder of the Quakers, was imprisoned here (and at other places too). The castle used to be called Dunheved (fort on the headland); Launceston derives from Llan Stefan (the church of Stephen).

Launceston, locally pronounced 'Lahnson', dominates the crossing of the London–Penzance road (A30) with the Bideford–Plymouth road (A388), as well as several villages and the River Tamar. Thus it could well be described as the gateway to Cornwall. It is in the care of the Department of the Environment and is open:
15 March–15 October 9.30 a.m.–6.30 p.m. daily including Sunday;
16 October–14 March 9.30 a.m.–4 p.m.
Closed Maundy Thursday, Good Friday, 24, 25, 26 December and 1 January.

PENDENNIS

Pendennis is an excellent example of sixteenth-century (and later) fortification. Henry VIII built the central keep, which is a circular building, and Elizabeth I built the surrounding bastions of the curtain. The keep has three storeys, 16 feet thick walls, and is 35 feet high.

The castle stood a six-month siege by Parliamentary forces in 1646. The Governor, Colonel John Arundell, was seventy, but defended the castle with such vigour and spirit that he was allowed to march out with the honours of war –

1 mile south-east of Falmouth, overlooking the inlet, its companion castle was St Mawes on the opposite side of the bay. The castle is in the care of the Department of the Environment and is open:
15 March–15 October, 9.30 a.m.–6.30 p.m. daily including Sunday;
16 October–14 March, 9.30 a.m.–4 p.m.

colours flying, trumpets blowing, and arms being carried. However, the long siege had taken its toll of the garrison, some of whom died soon afterwards.

As a coastal defence fort the castle was strengthened in the eighteenth and nineteenth centuries and used in World Wars I and II. Truly a fighting castle.

Closed Maundy Thursday, Good Friday, 24, 25, 26 December and 1 January. Tea in grounds in summer.

RESTORMEL

Restormel is an impressive example of a shell-keep. It is 125 feet in diameter, surrounded by a moat which was 50 feet wide; this is now dry.

Strategically, Restormel controls the Fowey river-valley from the west bank. The exterior wall is very well preserved and it is possible to see the outline of the interior buildings. Apart from its historical and military interest, it is an extremely beautiful ruin.

The first defences here were made by Baldwin FitzTurstin in the eleventh century. The site became part of the possessions of the Earls (later Dukes) of Cornwall, but was neglected and became ruinous in the fourteenth century. In the Civil War it was occupied and defended by a Parliamentary army, but was lost to a Royalist force commanded by Sir Richard Greville (1644). Later it became completely overgrown, but now this interesting castle is clear and open to view.

Restormel is 1½ miles north of Lostwithiel on the A390. It is in the care of the Department of the Environment and open: 15 March–15 October, 9.30 a.m.–6.30 p.m. daily including Sunday; 16 October–14 March, 9.30 a.m.–4 p.m. Closed Maundy Thursday, Good Friday, 24, 25, 26 December and 1 January.

ST MAWES

St Mawes is a Henry VIII castle, built to counter a possible French invasion. It was captured by Parliamentary forces in the Civil War without a shot being fired, mainly because an attack from the landward side had not been contemplated. It was manned in World Wars I and II, but now is in civilian care again. Like other Henry VIII forts it is remarkably complete.

2 miles from Falmouth, across the estuary. Companion castle to Pendennis. In the care of the Department of the Environment and open: 15 March–15 October, 9.30 a.m.–6.30 p.m. daily including Sunday; 16 October–14 March, 9.30 a.m.–4 p.m. Closed Maundy Thursday, Good Friday, 24, 25, 26 December and 1 January.

St Michael's Mount

This was originally a Benedictine priory, but its military value was too obvious for it to be left in the hands of monks. It was captured, by a ruse, by Henry de Pomeroy in the reign of Richard I, in the hope that John would succeed to the throne and approve the annexation, but the plan went awry. It was captured in the Wars of the Roses by the Earl of Oxford. It withstood a siege in the Civil War before being captured by the Parliamentarians.

The castle is on a pyramid of rock in Mount's Bay Marazion, ½ mile from the shore but connected by a causeway. Marazion is 3 miles east of Penzance on the A394.
Opening times:
1 April–31 May, Monday, Wednesday, Friday,
1 June–31 October, Monday, Tuesday, Wednesday, Friday, 10.30 a.m.–4.45 p.m.
1 November–31 March, Monday, Wednesday, Friday. Conducted tours only at 11 a.m., 12, 2, 3, 4 p.m.
Café and tea gardens in summer only.

St Michael's Mount

Tintagel

Tintagel (the site, not the ruined castle) is closely associated with King Arthur, the sixth-century warrior who seems to have based his anti-Saxon activities on Cornwall. Many myths and legends were woven around this romantic figure; now, perhaps unfortunately, they have contributed to building up a huge tourist souvenir industry.

The castle was originally built in 1145, on a rocky spur in a highly defensible position. Sea and weather have so eroded the site that the castle now looks as if it was built in two pieces. Another confusing fact is the presence of the remains of a Celtic monastery (possibly fourth century).

There is no other castle like Tintagel, and to visit it is an unusual experience. Apart from the beauty of the rugged site, there is a feeling of mystery and the supernatural which never seems far away in Cornwall.

20 miles from Bodmin, 5 miles north-west of Camelford, a half mile from Trevenna village.
The castle is in the care of the Department of the Environment and open:
15 March–15 October, 9.30 a.m.–6.30 p.m. daily including Sunday;
16 October–14 March 9.30 a.m.–4 p.m.
Closed Maundy Thursday, Good Friday, 24, 25, 26 December and 1 January.

CUMBRIA

Cumbria was formed in 1974 from Cumberland and Westmorland with strips of Lancashire and Yorkshire added. It contains some of the most impressive and beautiful scenery in the British Isles, the great lakes (which helped to inspire Coleridge and Wordsworth), and part of the Pennines – the 'backbone of England'. Cumberland wrestling, fell-running, cock-fighting, and Homeric contests with bare fists or cudgels were typical of the rugged scene. People needed to be tough in Cumbria in former days for Scots raiders would race over the border to lay about them – sometimes retaliating for raids on themselves, sometimes not. The archers of Kendal were a renowned military élite.

BROUGH

The site, important for controlling a crossing of the Pennines, had been fortified in Roman times. The first Norman castle was begun in the eleventh century and was greatly added to in the thirteenth and fourteenth. In the fifteenth century it was owned by Lord Clifford, nicknamed 'The Butcher' from his cruelties during the Wars of the Roses. He is said to have killed the Earl of Rutland, seventeen-year-old son of the Duke of York, after the Battle of Wakefield. He himself was killed shortly afterwards. His side (the Lancastrians of the Red Rose) lost the war and Clifford's son was brought up secretly as a shepherd's boy. Subsequently he became a noted scholar. The castle was restored, then damaged again, but is now in excellent repair.

On the A66 (Appleby–Barnard Castle), 8 miles from Appleby.
In the care of the Department of the Environment and open:
15 March–15 October, 9.30 a.m.–6.30 p.m. daily including Sunday;
16 October–14 March, 9.30 a.m.–4 p.m.
Closed Maundy Thursday, Good Friday, 24, 25, 26 December and 1 January.

Brough

BROUGHAM

The Romans had a large fort here, but the present castle was probably begun in the twelfth century by Hugh d'Albini. In the thirteenth century it passed through marriage to the notorious Cliffords (*see* Brough *above*). It was repaired in the seventeenth century by Lady Anne Clifford – to whom the country is indebted for the restoration of other castles as well – but her grandson was less responsibly minded and sold off parts of Brougham for building material. There is a lot to see at Brougham, ruined though it is.

1½ miles east of Penrith on the A66.
Department of the Environment.
Open:
15 March–15 October, 9.30 a.m.–6.30 p.m. daily including Sunday;
16 October–14 March, 9.30 a.m.–4 p.m.
Closed Maundy Thursday, Good Friday, 24, 25, 26 December and 1 January.

Brougham

CARLISLE

The first building was begun by William Rufus with a view to holding off the Scots; but it was not always successful. Its finest hour was in 1314 when the Scots were in high spirits after their great victory at Bannockburn.

All attempts to reduce Carlisle Castle failed, and the Scots had to retire disappointed. Few castles have seen as much action; in the Middle Ages, in the Civil War, and in the 1743 rising it was always in the thick of the fight. Unfortunately its position near the city centre eventually caused it to lose

The castle is in the town itself at the north end.
Department of the Environment.
Open:
March and October, Weekdays, 9.30 a.m.–5.30 p.m.
Sundays 2–5.30 p.m.
April, daily 9.30 a.m.–5.30 p.m.
May–September, daily 9.30 a.m.–7 p.m.

Carlisle

more masonry and territory from depredation than from all its former battles. Even so, there is much to see. It houses the museum of the King's Own Border Regiment.

November and February, weekdays 9.30 a.m.–4 p.m. Sundays, 2–4 p.m. Closed Maundy Thursday, Good Friday, 24, 25, 26 December and 1 January.

MUNCASTER

Originally a simple square tower built on Roman foundation. Castle dates back to thirteenth century. Present house, which incorporates the castle, was built by Salvin. Superb collection of tapestries, china, pictures (including Gainsborough, Velazquez, Van Dyck) and furniture.

1½ miles south-east of Ravenglass on the A495. Privately owned. Open as follows: Grounds and Bird Garden: 4 April–5 October, daily except Friday, but open Good Friday 12 noon–5 p.m. Castle: 4 April–5 October Tuesday, Wednesday, Thursday and Sunday 2–5 p.m. (last admission 4.30 p.m.) Lunch, tea, etc available.

SIZERGH

Sizergh has been the home of the Strickland family for 700 years. Basically it is a Peel tower dating from 1340, but there are attached buildings. The Stricklands have a fine record of service to their country from Agincourt in 1415 to the present day. An early member of the family married into the family which later would produce George Washington. There is a magnificent old sword here as well as portraits and other exhibits.

3½ miles south of Kendal north-west of A6/A591 interchange. Open: April–28 September. Wednesday and Sundays, also 29 May and Thursdays in July and August 2–5.45 p.m.

DERBYSHIRE

Derbyshire is renowned for its spas (Buxton and Matlock), for Rolls-Royce, for mineral mines, for scenery (particularly the Peak District), for the Burton-on-Trent beers, and for the famous fishermen Charles Cotton and Isaac Walton. Eyam, the village which was completely wiped out by the great plague of 1665-6, is in Derbyshire and so too are the great country houses Chatsworth and Haddon Hall, both close to Bakewell and open to the public.

PEVERIL

William Peveril began the castle in 1090, but the square tower which may be seen today was built in 1176. Later it was owned by Simon de Montfort, by young Prince Edward who became Edward III, and by John de Warenne, Earl of Surrey. Although it seems to have had no military adventures, it was always important because of the nearby lead mines. Anyone wishing to acquire those illegally would have to reckon with Peveril. Sir Walter Scott made it well known by his novel *Peveril of the Peak*.

On the A652 at Castleton. The visitor parks his car in the village below and makes a considerable though graduated climb. Department of the Environment.
Open:
15 March–15 October, 9.30 a.m.–6.30 p.m. daily including Sundays,
16 October–14 March, 9.30 a.m.–4 p.m.
Closed Maundy Thursday, Good Friday, 24, 25, 26 December and 1 January.

Peveril

DEVONSHIRE

Devonshire is the third largest county in England but is not very heavily populated. Drake, Hawkins and Raleigh, Dartmoor, prehistoric antiquities, Robert Herrick the poet and Joshua Reynolds the painter, magnificent scenery and little seaside villages, and the famous Devon regiment which held back fifteen times its own number in World War I, are all part of the story of Devon.

BERRY POMEROY

Berry Pomeroy is a haunted castle. This may amuse the sceptics, but they may be less amused if they are in the ruins after dusk than they will be when they are back in their hotel again. Berry Pomeroy, although in Devon, belongs to the Dukes of Somerset. The builders and holders of the first castle were the family of de la Pomerai, who came over with the Conqueror. However, they lost it in 1549 after an unsuccessful rebellion, and it went to the Seymours, Dukes of Somerset, who built extensively. Between 1688 and 1701 the castle was burnt in a fire – some say the castle was struck by lightning. Even after this mysterious disaster there are plenty of ruins to see, but the visitor is advised to pick his way carefully.

One of the ghosts is Margaret de Pomeroy who was starved to death by her sister; they both loved the same man. This is a ghost which it is profoundly unlucky to see. Another woman walks through the woods. She is supposed to have smothered her illegitimate baby. Yet another woman who haunts the castle was caught in a secret assignation by her brother who killed the guilty pair. From much farther back, in the late twelfth century, comes the ghost of Henry de Pomerai, who killed a herald but later stabbed himself to death. Rather more material relics came from the nearby crossroads, where at one time there was a gibbet. Workmen used to dig up skulls of men who had been hanged on it.

Take the A385 from Totnes to Torbay, but turn off at True Street. Go through Berry Pomeroy village towards Afton. The castle is on the left; it is about 3½ miles from Totnes. As it is not easy to find, an Ordnance Survey map is useful. Sheet 202, Torbay and Dartmoor, 1:5000, shows it at grid reference 839 625.
The castle is open 10 a.m.–6 p.m. every day, and there is a convenient car park.

CASTLE DROGO

Drogo has the distinction of being the most modern castle listed in this book. As the kitchens and the chapel are dug into the rock, it might seem an eminently suitable castle for the nuclear age. It was built between 1910 and 1930 by Sir Edwin Lutyens and has remarkable views.

2 miles north-east of Chagford; 1 mile south of the A30. National Trust. Open 1 April–31 October, daily 11 a.m.–6 p.m. Lunch and tea available.

COMPTON

Compton was built by a Gilbert in 1329, but is more of a defensible manor-house than castle. The Gilberts have lived here almost continuously ever since. Unfortunately, it was sold in the nineteenth century and the owner of the time altered the structure considerably; the present owner has done much to restore it. Sir Humphrey Gilbert, who claimed Newfoundland on behalf of Queen Elizabeth I, was a member of this family; he was half-brother to that other famous Elizabethan explorer, Sir Walter Raleigh (*see* Sherborne Castle).

Compton is just off the A381 between Newton Abbot and Totnes. It is owned by the National Trust and is open on Mondays, Wednesdays and Thursdays from 10 a.m. to noon and from 2 to 5 p.m. (It should not be confused with Compton Castle in Somerset, which is privately owned.)

DARTMOUTH

Dartmouth was an important port in the Middle Ages and there was a small castle on this site, but the present building is the result of a raid in 1404, when a French army, said to number 6,000, attacked Dartmouth. A chain was later stretched across the harbour mouth, soon to be followed by the building of the present castle, although that proved a lengthy process. The castle was designed for guns. However, the large number of existing gun loops owes more to later problems than to the medieval French invasions. Surprisingly enough, in the seventeenth century there was a threat from Moroccan pirates. The castle saw heavy fighting in the Civil War, but was too valuable strategically to be demolished. In 1940 it was used for local defence, like Pevensey and Portchester (or Porchester).

Dartmouth castle is in a dominating position overlooking the bay from the hillside and approached along the B3025. It is in the care of the Department of the Environment and open: 15 March–15 October, 9.30 a.m.–6.30 p.m. daily including Sundays; 16 October–14 March, 9.30 a.m.–4 p.m. Closed Maundy Thursday, Good Friday, 24, 25, 26 December and 1 January.

LYDFORD

Lydford was apparently fortified from early times, but the present ruins mainly date from the thirteenth century. However, the fact that Lydford Castle also housed a court and a prison in an area where lawlessness was dealt with summarily and extremely harshly gave it a reputation which extended well beyond Devonshire. 'The law of Lydford' meant summary justice, thus the doggerel:

> First hang, then draw
> Then hear the cause by Lydford law.

and by another versifier referring to the cramped conditions:

> To lie therein one night 'tis guessed
> 'Twere better to be stoned and pressed
> Or hanged, now choose you whether.

Lydford Bridge also has a sinister reputation, mainly for suicides. Yet, Lydford was once a small town, had a mint, and was part of the possessions of Richard, Earl of Cornwall.

Lydford is 8 miles from Tavistock and is open at all times. The site is cared for by the Department of the Environment.

OKEHAMPTON

Okehampton is an interesting example of how a castle can be saved from total ruin. Before the Government took it over it was so overgrown and decayed that it was considered 'unvisitable'. Today there is much of interest to see.

The first castle was built in the eleventh century, but was doubtless of wood. The keep is thirteenth century and was built by Hugh Courtenay. It is a curious fortification, for many of the buildings appear to have been sited purely for domestic reasons and without regard to defence. Okehampton's decay began in 1538 when its owner Henry Courtenay, Marquis of Exeter, was beheaded for being involved in a plot against Henry VIII. Fortunately, the decline of Okehampton has now been checked.

The castle lies 1 mile south-west of Okehampton. It is in the care of the Department of the Environment and open:
15 March–15 October, 9.30 a.m.–6.30 p.m. daily including Sunday;
16 October–14 March, 9.30 a.m.–4 p.m. Closed Maundy Thursday, Good Friday, 24, 25, 26 December and 1 January.

POWDERHAM

Powderham was built by the Courtenays, who have been the Earls of Devon for 600 years. The original castle was built in 1390, but it was extended and strengthened later. The Courtenays were in trouble during the first half of the sixteenth century, but retained the castle. During the Civil War it was a Royalist stronghold, but eventually surrendered to the Parliamentary forces in 1646. It was not slighted, as the Courtenays were related to a Parliamentary general. In the eighteenth century it was remodelled to make it a palatial mansion.

8 miles south-west of Exeter on the A379 to Dawlish. Owned by the Earl and Countess of Devon. (There are, separately, a Duke of Devonshire and an Earl of Devon; the reasons are too long and complicated to set out here).
Open to the public Easter Sunday and Monday, then 13 April–18 May on Sundays;
19 May–28 September, daily, except Fridays and Saturdays, 2–6 p.m.
Restaurant. Varied entertainments such as falconry, ancient fairs, horse trials etc on occasions.

TIVERTON

Built in 1106 for Henry I by Richard de Redvers, First Earl of Devon. Medieval tower and gatehouse. Fine furniture and portraits of Joan of Arc and her relatives.

On the outskirts of Tiverton by St Peter's Church.
National Trust.
Open:
Easter; 5–9 April, 18 May–25 September daily (except Fridays and Saturdays) 2.30–5.30 p.m.

TOTNES

Totnes Castle is an excellent example of a motte and bailey castle with a shell-keep (other shell-keeps in the West Country are Restormel and Trematon). In view of the disputes, mainly legal and bloodless, over the ownership of the castle and the long periods of complete neglect it has experienced, it is amazing that Totnes is so complete and well preserved. In spite of its valuable strategic position, commanding the River Dart at a point where three valleys join, it appears to have seen very little action. In the local shops it is possible to buy postcards that show (imaginatively) what it was like in its heyday; they are interesting, but the visitor will find plenty to impress him in its present state.

Totnes Castle is on the edge of an attractive Devonshire town and can be seen from afar. It is in the care of the Department of the Environment and open:
15 March–15 October, 9.30 a.m.–6.30 p.m. daily including Sunday;
16 October–14 March, 9.30 a.m.–4 p.m.
Closed Maundy Thursdays, Good Friday, 24, 25, 26 December and 1 January.

DORSET

Dorset is a quiet and unspoilt county but the thought that oil is now being extracted there gives some doubt about the endurance of tranquillity. However, harmony does not always reside in a quiet country setting, as the novels of Thomas Hardy show, and one is reminded of Dorset's military connections by the firing range at Lulworth and the proving grounds at Studland Bay.

Bournemouth became part of Dorset when it was included in the county by the 1974 boundary changes. At the other end of the Dorset coast is Lyme Regis which was an important seaport in the Middle Ages. There are many impressive earthworks but the most striking is Maiden Castle, two miles south-west of Dorchester, off the A354. Maiden Castle was probably begun 3,000 years ago but most of the work on the vast earth ramparts and deep ditches, both originally reinforced by stakes, was completed in the Iron Age (900 BC – 100 BC). Maiden Castle is not difficult of access and should not be missed.

Another interesting earthwork in Dorset is the tenth-century ramparts at Wareham. They are a reminder of what life was like in less settled times.

CHRISTCHURCH

Christchurch was an unlucky castle for some of its owners, several of whom were beheaded. It saw vigorous action in the Civil War. The original castle dates back to the twelfth century. There is not much left but what there is is interesting.

The remains of the castle are in the garden of the King's Arms Hotel, but it is open at the normal Department of the Environment times:
15 March–15 October, 9.30 a.m.–6.30 p.m. daily including Sunday;
16 October–14 March, 9.30 a.m.–4 p.m.
Closed Maundy Thursday, Good Friday, 24, 25, 26 December and 1 January.

CORFE

There was a manor here in the tenth century and it was the scene of the treacherous murder of Edward, son of King Edgar, in 978. He had called for a cup of wine when hunting and it was brought by his stepmother. As he drank, one of her retainers stabbed him in the back. Her own son, Ethelred the Unready, then became king and the worst king in British history.

The stone keep is twelfth century and there were many additions in the twelfth and thirteenth centuries. During the Civil War it was defended for

On the A351 halfway between Swanage and Wareham. The castle stands on a hill and is visible for miles around. It is open from Easter until 1 October from 10 a.m. until evening. From 2 October to the following Easter it is open from 2 p.m. until evening. Tea may be obtained in the village.

the Royalists by Lady Bankes when her husband was serving with the King's army elsewhere. She showed great resolution in the face of determined gunfire and mining and the siege was abandoned. Three years later, when she was away herself, it was again attacked and this time was betrayed. It was heavily slighted by the Parliamentary forces but recently much work has been done on it to make it safe for visitors. There are extensive ruins and they are both impressive and memorable.

Corfe

PORTLAND

This is a Henry VIII castle, dating from approximately 1540. It saw no action until the Civil War when it was seized by Royalists in 1642, lost twice the same year and finally handed over to Parliament in 1646. On one occasion it was captured by Royalists by a ruse. A party wearing Parliamentarian colours galloped up to the castle hotly pursued by Royalists. The gates were flung open to let them in – but once inside they showed their true colours as Royalists and captured the castle. Portland is a strong castle with plenty of gunports; it has often been used for military and naval purposes but is now in civilian hands again.

The castle is on the northern shore of the Isle of Portland. It is in the care of the Department of the Environment and open:
15 March–15 October, 9.30 a.m.–6.30 p.m. daily including Sunday;
16 October–14 March, 9.30 a.m.–4 p.m.
Closed Maundy Thursday, Good Friday, 24, 25, 26 December and 1 January.

SHERBORNE

Sherborne old castle is a ruin, but an interesting one; Sherborne new castle is a sixteenth-century mansion which has been in the continuous occupation of the Digby family since 1617. The former was besieged twice during the Civil War; in the first siege the Royalists beat off their Parliamentary opponents, but in the second a tremendous bombardment battered the castle into surrender.

The new castle was begun by Sir Walter Raleigh. It is said that once when he was sitting in his garden here, trying out his new discovery – tobacco – a servant threw water over him believing that he was on fire.

There are two Sherborne castles but they are close together, east of the town, off the A30. The old castle is in the care of the Department of the Environment and open:
15 March–15 October, 9.30 a.m.–6.30 p.m. daily including Sunday;
16 October–14 March, 9.30 a.m.–4 p.m.
Closed Maundy Thursday, Good Friday, 24, 25, 26 December and 1 January.
The new castle is open from Easter Saturday to the last Sunday in September on Thursdays, Saturdays, Sundays and Bank Holiday Mondays 2–6 p.m. Tea is available.

DURHAM

Durham has a long history of repelling invasions, for it lay on one of the main routes into England from the north. However, in 1974 it was distinctly less successful and lost land to the north to the new county of Tyne and Wear, and to the south to help make Cleveland.

The first Norman Bishop of Durham (in the eleventh century) was a fighting man of distinction whose power extended widely. Medieval bishops were considerably more warlike than their successors – Bishop Odo, of Kent, who came over with William the Conqueror, eventually led a rebellion against William II. Roger, Bishop of Salisbury in 1139, left his mistress 'at home' to defend Devizes castle (which she did very well) while he conducted a rebellion elsewhere. Ecclesiastical law forbade bishops to carry swords in battle so that they would not shed blood; instead they carried a murderous weapon called a mace which probably did even more damage.

BARNARD CASTLE

For the visitor, Barnard Castle does not compare with such castles as Bamburgh or Alnwick, but in its day it was probably nearly as powerful. It stands on a well-chosen site on the banks of the Tees and, although a ruin, is extensive enough to keep the visitor busy with detective work identifying the former strongpoints. It dates from the mid-twelfth century when Bernard or Barnard Bailleul decided to fortify it. One of the Bailleuls (or Balliols) founded Balliol College, Oxford. It was involved in various wars and endless disputes between the owners and the Bishops of Durham. It was defended by the Vanes for the Royalists during the Civil War, but eventually fell to Roundhead cannonfire. An unusual feature of the castle is that it has four baileys.

Barnard Castle is in the middle of the town of that name, so there is no problem in finding it. It is in the care of the Department of the Environment and open:
15 March–15 October, 9.30 a.m.–6.30 p.m. daily including Sunday;
16 October–14 March, 9.30 a.m.–4 p.m.
Closed Maundy Thursday, Good Friday, 24, 25, 26 December and 1 January.

Barnard

DURHAM

The castle began as a wooden building in 1072 and three years later successfully beat off an attack by Danes. The gatehouse is twelfth century and most of the other buildings fourteenth century. It was given to the university in the nineteenth century. There are interesting paintings and there is a good collection of armour. The nearby cathedral is typical of strong, military style, Norman architecture. Together, castle and cathedral are a fine example of the Norman military/ecclesiastical partnership.

Durham Castle is in the centre of the city, and stands alongside the cathedral, which is one of the most impressive in the country. The best view of the castle is from below, where it overlooks the River Wear, but it is also possible to see the interior at certain times.

The visiting hours are slightly complicated by the fact that the castle houses Durham University. However, visitors are welcome from 1 April to 21 April, and in July, August and September from 10 a.m. to 12 noon and from 2 to 4.30 p.m. on weekdays. For the rest of the year they are welcome on Mondays, Wednesdays and Saturdays from 2 to 4 p.m.

Durham

LUMLEY

The castle was built in the late fourteenth century by Ralph, or Robert, Lumley. The Lumleys often backed the losing side and suffered accordingly, but they held on to the castle. In the eighteenth century Vanbrugh rebuilt parts of the castle, making it a palatial mansion – where visitors may enjoy medieval banquets.

Today, it has become a luxury hotel with television in all bedrooms and even facilities for helicopter landing. The banquets are voluntary. For those preferring more up-to-date menus there is a very high standard of conventional fare. Visitors should telephone (Chester-le-Street) 0385 3267.

Lumley is 1 mile south of Chester-le-Street.

RABY

Castle and gardens are magnificent; the former being full of fine furniture and pictures, the latter extending over ten acres. The castle was built by the mighty Nevilles, ancestors of Warwick the Kingmaker, in the fourteenth century. The Nevilles were one of the most powerful baronial families who had built up their fortunes by dynastic marriages. In the Civil War, Raby had a busy time and changed hands twice. It does not look particularly defensible today, but this is because the moats have been emptied and a high curtain wall and outworks demolished.

1 mile north of Staindrop on the A688 (Barnard Castle–Bishop Auckland). It is owned by Lord Barnard, and is open to the public at the following times:
Easter weekend: Saturday–Tuesday; then 9 April–29 June Wednesdays and Sundays.
1 July–30 September, daily except Saturday.
Also 5 May and Spring and Autumn Bank Holiday weekends Saturday–Tuesday.
Hours 2–5 p.m.
Tea in the former stables.

Raby

overleaf—Castle Hedingham

ESSEX

Essex was once the place of the East Saxons – Sussex was the place of the South Saxons, and there were other settlements in Middlesex and Wessex. Although a small county, Essex has great variety. It has been famous for its oysters, its silk, its beer, and around Saffron Walden (where there are the remains of a once powerful castle) there were fields of saffron which was used much more widely in the Middle Ages to dye food yellow than it is today. Medieval cooks liked to colour their foods and would dye them green with mint, yellow with saffron, black with charcoal or red with sanders, a red dye made from sandalwood. Pork was often coloured green!

CASTLE HEDINGHAM

This is a twelfth-century Norman castle with a huge three-storey keep; it was immensely strong and once had a bailey three acres in extent. It was owned by the de Veres, Earls of Oxford, who seem to have been unduly accident-prone. One helped lose the Battle of Barnet (1471) for his side by going astray in the fog; he spent many years in prison but eventually was released and was 'called on' by Henry VII at Hedingham. He turned out all his retainers in honour of the occasion and was fined over £10,000 by his mean-minded monarch for having too many men in uniform.

Castle Hedingham is 4 miles north of Halstead, just off the A604. Although privately owned it is open to the public on Bank Holidays 10 a.m.–6 p.m. and from May to September on Tuesdays, Thursdays and Saturdays 2–6 p.m.

COLCHESTER

The castle was built in the late eleventh century by Eudo, who was a dapifer, or steward, of William I, William II and Henry I. He sited it within the old Roman city. On his death on 1120 it passed to the Crown. It was involved in King John's war in 1215, and again in the Civil War in 1648. It has the largest keep in Europe – for it still measures 171 feet by 146 feet. It is now only two storeys high but once had a third storey.

Colchester Castle, which is in the town, houses the Colchester and Essex Museum and is open on weekdays 10 a.m.–5 p.m. On Sundays in the summer it is open 2.30–5 p.m. It is possible to go on a tour of the vaults and cells on weekdays.

HADLEIGH

The castle was begun by Hubert de Burgh in 1231

Hadleigh Castle is just south

but he soon lost it to the Crown. Henry III completed the buildings, and although it is now a ruin there is much to see. Henry VIII's discarded wife, Anne of Cleves, whom he referred to as his 'Flanders Mare' on account of her unattractive appearance, lived here after the divorce. Apparently she occupied herself placidly with needlework. The castle, a favourite subject of painters, achieved extra fame when Constable made it one of his subjects.

of the village of Hadleigh, and 1 mile west of Leigh-on-Sea. It is in the care of the Department of the Environment and open:
15 March–15 October, 9.30 a.m.–6.30 p.m. daily including Sunday;
16 October–14 March, 9.30 a.m.–4 p.m.
Closed Maundy Thursday, Good Friday, 24, 25, 26 December and 1 January.

Pleshey

PLESHEY

Pleshey was once a large castle but today much has disappeared, although the tall motte and the moat remain. Its history has been violent. It was begun by the notorious Mandevilles and passed to the Bohuns. In 1397 the Duke of Gloucester, who owned it at that time, was decoyed to Calais and murdered by the orders of his nephew, Richard II. Richard seized the castle's goods which included 'a great bed of gold'. Later Richard was deposed and disappeared, presumably at Pontefract, but a headstone bearing the inscription Richard II was found at Pleshey later. Perhaps he was murdered here; it is an intriguing mystery.

Pleshey Castle, near Chelmsford, is open to the public at all times.

GLOUCESTERSHIRE/AVON

Gloucestershire extends from the Midlands to the West Country, and includes Cotswold villages and part of the River Severn. The Earls and, later, Dukes of Gloucester have figured constantly in English history, for good or ill. Duke Humphrey (1391–1447) was a man of culture who left his own books to a library at Oxford University – today they comprise the oldest part of the Bodleian Library which came into existence more than a hundred and fifty years after Humphrey's death. Robert, natural son of Henry I, was a loyal supporter of his half-sister Matilda in the anarchical wars of the twelfth century; Gilbert, the 'Red Earl', first supported then fought against Simon de Montfort (*see* Kenilworth); Richard, the alleged hunchback, who was killed at Bosworth in 1485, was probably the most notorious Gloucester. He was said to have reached the throne by a series of murders, including that of Henry VI and the Princes in the Tower, but not everyone agrees on his guilt. Yet today there is no castle at Gloucester (although there is a magnificent cathedral) and the military role is taken up by aircraft.

BERKELEY

This is the oldest inhabited castle in England and the present owner is Major R. J. G. Berkeley.

It houses superb furniture and paintings and is surrounded by most attractive gardens; but for many people the attraction of Berkeley is the room where Edward II was murdered (1327) with a red-hot poker. His cell, then a foul dungeon, now looks quite comfortable. In 1470 the Berkeleys had a private war with their neighbours, quite apart from the Wars of the Roses which were then at their height. During the Civil War it was occupied by both sides, but was not seriously slighted afterwards.

The castle is on the outskirts of the unspoilt little town of Berkeley, which lies midway between Bristol and Gloucester, just off the A38. It is open daily except Mondays, from May to August 11 a.m.–5 p.m. (Sundays 2–5 p.m.) and in April weekdays (except Mondays) 2–5 p.m. September daily 2–5 p.m. except Mondays. October, Sundays only 2–4.30 p.m. Bank Holidays Monday 2–5 p.m. Tea available.

ST BRIAVELS

The remains of a twelfth-century castle, with an interesting gatehouse. Some dark deeds occurred here according to legend.

At St Briavels. In the care of the Department of the Environment and open: 15 March–15 October, 9.30 a.m.–6.30 p.m. daily including Sunday; 16 October–14 March, 9.30 a.m.–4 p.m. Closed Maundy Thursday, Good Friday, 24, 25, 26 December and 1 January.

Sudeley

SUDELEY

Much of Sudeley is nineteenth century but some of it dates from the fourteenth century. It was the home of Catherine Parr, the sixth wife of Henry VIII, who survived him but apparently was lucky to do so. Later, she married Thomas Seymour who, after her death, was executed, as was Catherine's own brother, for allegedly engaging in various plots.

The castle was captured and recaptured in the Civil War. Today, restored, it has much for the visitor.

6 miles north-east of Cheltenham on the A46. Open March to October daily 12 noon–5.30 p.m. Tea in restaurant.

THORNBURY (COUNTY OF AVON)

The castle was erected in 1511 by the Duke of Buckingham and is the last defensible/residential castle to be built in England. It is an attractive building, but the owner never lived to see it completed because he was executed by Henry VIII in 1512 for alleged treason. It seems that Buckingham kept a large private army, which was quartered here, and felt that this would enable him to overawe his critics.

Thornbury is just off the B4461 on the edge of Alveston. Viewing the castle is made slightly difficult by the fact that it has now been converted into a high-class restaurant where it is necessary to book well ahead. Many visitors may, of course, wish to do this.

HAMPSHIRE

With ports like Southampton and Portsmouth at its southern end and Winchester in the middle it is not surprising that Hampshire has played a leading part in English history. Winchester is an example of a commercial town acquiring military importance in spite of, rather than because of, its site. But little remains of Winchester's two castles, one in the town centre, and the other at Wolvesey on the southern outskirts. Winchester's chief glory is its cathedral and nearby college. William Rufus is buried here. It is said that the tower fell down soon afterwards showing divine displeasure at the burial of such a godless man; others blamed the Norman architects. The cathedral stood for some six hundred years on a raft of logs in a swamp but is now supported by a modern foundation. Hampshire has chalk streams, the Itchen and the Avon, famous for trout-fishing.

HURST

Hurst is a Henry VIII castle, like Deal and Walmer, and was built in the early 1540s. It is substantial, and in World Wars I and II was manned again.

During the Civil War, Hurst was held for Parliament and was not attacked. Charles I was brought here from Carisbrooke before his trial in 1648, but does not appear to have been very comfortably accommodated.

Modifications have made it difficult to visualise the castle as it was originally, but the alterations for later use are themselves of considerable interest.

Hurst is at the end of a 2½ mile spit of shingle and can be walked to at low tide, but it is usually approached by ferry from Keyhaven. Hurst is in the care of the Department of the Environment and open:
15 March–15 October, 9.30 a.m.–6.30 p.m. daily including Sunday;
16 October–14 March, 9.30 a.m.–4 p.m.
Closed Maundy Thursday, Good Friday, 24, 25, 26 December and 1 January.

PORTCHESTER

This is a fine Norman castle inside an old Roman fort. It is possible to walk all round the well-preserved Roman walls, examine the bastion towers, and ascend to the upper floors of the restored castle.

The Roman fort is third century and was built for the same reason as Pevensey – to beat off Saxon raiders. The 18 feet walls, complete all round, are a fine sight, much beloved by photographers. Henry I built the keep with its 12 feet thick walls. Both were strengthened later. It was visited by various monarchs, and Henry V sailed from here when he set out to conquer

6 miles from Portsmouth on the outskirts of the attractive village of Portchester (sometimes written Porchester). In the care of the Department of the Environment and open:
15 March–15 October, 9.30 a.m.–6.30 p.m. daily including Sunday;
16 October–14 March, 9.30 a.m.–4 p.m.
Closed Maundy Thursday, Good Friday, 24, 25, 26 December and 1 January.

France. Its later history was less glamorous, for it housed Dutch prisoners in the seventeenth century and French prisoners during the Napoleonic Wars – 5,000 men could be 'accommodated'. Many died, mainly from malnutrition. It was said that a visitor once tied up his horse at the castle and when he returned an hour or two later found it had disappeared. It had already been eaten!

Porchester

HEREFORD AND WORCESTER

This cumbersome name was created in 1974 when Herefordshire and Worcester-shire were joined together. The former on the Welsh border, had a long history of fighting, but Hereford Castle has now completely gone. At one time, to kill a Welshman with an arrow within Hereford town walls was not a crime. The country is famed for salmon fishing on the Wye, for white-faced Hereford cattle and for productive farming, but there are many traces of fortifications dating from less settled times.

Worcestershire is renowned for the fruit of Evesham and the ruddy Worcester apple but has considerable manufacturing activities. Droitwich and Malvern are spas. Worcester castle was completely demolished and the mound removed in 1848.

GOODRICH

Goodrich seems to be somewhat off the beaten track, but in its day it commanded an ancient crossing-point of the River Wye. The Roman road from Gloucester to Caerleon-on-Usk seems to have passed through here, and undoubtedly this route was in use during the Middle Ages. The first Norman castle was built by Godric Mappestone in the eleventh century; hence Godric's or Goodrich castle. In the fourteenth century the castle came into the hands of the Talbots, Earls of Shrewsbury, a formidable fighting family. In the Civil War Goodrich passed from Parliamentary control to Royalist. It was twice besieged and on the second occasion, in 1646, was forced to surrender after the water-supply had been cut off. Although castles had wells it was not always possible to obtain enough water for drinking and extinguishing fires started by incendiary arrows. On occasion wine was used for the latter purpose.

There is a lot to see at Goodrich, ruined though it is. There is a massive keep and there are huge bastion towers, made immensely strong by sloping plinths.

Goodrich is just off the A40, 3 miles south-west of Ross-on-Wye. The approach is along a signposted footpath, but the visitor should not be put off by the thought of the $\frac{1}{2}$ mile walk which this involves. In the care of the Department of the Environmnt and open:
15 March–15 October, 9.30 a.m.–6.30 p.m. daily including Sunday;
16 October–14 March, 9.30 a.m.–4 p.m.
Closed Maundy Thursday, Good Friday, 24, 25, 26 December and 1 January.

HERTFORDSHIRE

In Hertfordshire is St Albans which the Romans kept as a military strongpoint. St Albans also saw two important battles in the fifteenth century Wars of the Roses. Medieval wall paintings were uncovered in the cathedral recently. Of the former Hertford castle the gatehouse has now become council offices surrounded by a few remains. Bishop's Stortford castle is now only a mound surrounded by a park.

BERKHAMSTED

Berkhamsted castle was begun soon after 1066 by William the Conqueror's half-brother, Robert of Mortain, but most of the present masonry dates from the twelfth and thirteenth centuries. The height of the walls and the massive earthwork immediately impress the visitor and would do so even more if the railway builders – the vandals of the nineteenth century – had not destroyed a gateway and barbican. Nevertheless, the castle looks so powerful that it is difficult to believe that it held out for only fourteen days against a siege in 1216. Apparently a continuous shower of heavy stones from giant mangonels proved too much.

Berkhamsted has housed some famous people; among them Thomas Becket, the Black Prince, Piers Gaveston, Anne Boleyn. It escaped damage during the Civil War, but was less lucky with predatory builders who were looking for stones to build houses.

The castle is a few hundred yards from the main street. It is in the care of the Department of the Environment and open:
15 March–15 October, 9.30 a.m.–6.30 p.m. daily including Sunday;
16 October–14 March, 9.30 a.m.–4 p.m.
Closed Maundy Thursday, Good Friday, 24, 25, 26 December and 1 January.

Berkhamsted

HUMBERSIDE

Humberside consists of a part of the old East Riding of Yorkshire and part of north Lincolnshire, territories separated by the Humber and, probably because of the rivalry between Grimsby and Hull, not particularly drawn to each other.

SKIPSEA

Skipsea is of interest because it is a large eleventh-century castle with substantial water defences. Although there is little to see except earthworks, an assessment of its military value can be made, and the castle will fascinate those who appreciate ingenuity in the use of water to extend a castle's outer defences.

At Hornsea. In the care of the Department of the Environment and open:
15 March–15 October, 9.30 a.m.–6.30 p.m. daily including Sunday;
16 October–14 March, 9.30 a.m.–4 p.m.
Closed Maundy Thursday, Good Friday, 24, 25, 26 December and 1 January.

Carisbrooke

ISLE OF WIGHT

The Isle of Wight is Britain in miniature. It is approximately twenty-five by forty miles in size and is separated from Portsmouth and Southampton by Spithead and the Solent. The crossing takes half an hour. The island has several excellent holiday resorts: Sandown, Shanklin, Ventnor and Ryde, and a great yachting mecca at Cowes. Queen Victoria used Osborne House as a residence, especially in the winter; it is now a convalescent home. The island saw some stirring naval battles in the Middle Ages and was once invaded and occupied by the French with 2,000 troops – but not for long.

CARISBROOKE

Carisbrooke saw plenty of fighting before the Normans built a castle in the eleventh century, and more action afterwards. It was involved in the twelfth-century war between Stephen and Matilda, in resisting a French invasion in 1377, and in the Wars of the Roses in the fifteenth century. It is probably best known for the fact that it housed Charles I as a prisoner in 1647. He made three attempts to escape, all of which were disastrous failures.

Princess Beatrice, Queen Victoria's youngest daughter, lived here from 1896 to 1951.

The castle contains a good museum, but a principal attraction is the well-house. The well is 161 feet deep and the rope is drawn by donkeys, who work in shifts; each drawing means a walk of 300 yards for the donkey.

Carisbrooke is within 2 miles of Newport, on the southern side. It is in the care of the Department of the Environment and open: 15 March–15 October 9.30 a.m.–6.30 p.m. daily including Sunday; 16 October–14 March, 9.30 a.m.–4 p.m. Closed Maundy Thursday, Good Friday, 24, 25, 26 December and 1 January.

YARMOUTH

Most people, on hearing 'Yarmouth', will immediately think of Norfolk, where they will find Caister near by. However, the Norfolk Yarmouth Castle was demolished three hundred years ago. The Isle of Wight castle is a Henry VIII castle but of somewhat unusual design. It has an arrow-head bastion which was the earliest one in England; the other bastions were semicircular. Yarmouth was, of course, altered and improved later to deal with other threats, such as the Napoleonic Wars. It was garrisoned in World Wars I and II.

The castle is in the town, behind the George Hotel. It is a Department of the Environment castle and open: 15 March–15 October, 9.30 a.m.–6.30 p.m. daily including Sunday; 16 October–14 March, 9.30 a.m.–4 p.m. Closed Maundy Thursday, Good Friday, 24, 25, 26 December and 1 January.

KENT

Kent is known as the 'Garden of England' because of its orchards, its hop fields and its rural appearance. However, north Kent along the Thames Estuary is industrialised and not pretty. Kent has seen more of fighting and attempted invasions than most counties. Dover was nicknamed 'Hellfire Corner' in World War II because of the endless bombing it sustained. Much of the aerial Battle of Britain was fought in the Kent skies. In World War I the famous 'Dover Patrol' kept the route clear to France when some ten million troops were ferried back and forth. Canterbury has the magnificent cathedral and its precincts. Kent is also famed for light-hearted but successful cricket. A 'Man of Kent' lives east of the Medway and a Kentishman lives west of it. 'Kentish Rag' is a hard limestone most suitable for building castles. 'Kentish Fire' is the rhythmic applause designed to stop any orator from continuing. Tonbridge castle, once so powerful, is only a fragment of its former size but still has the thirteenth-century gatehouse, and the site is worth seeing; Cooling Castle, a mile east of Cliffe, is privately owned but can be seen from the road; at West Malling is St Leonard's Tower, which is all that remains of a bigger castle. The A228 passes it and it is open at all times.

Kent has many magnificent houses which lie outside the scope of this book. Knole, Penshurst and Chartwell are places which a visitor to Kent should try to see.

ALLINGTON

Allington has a long history. There is said to have been a fortification on the site soon after the Conquest, perhaps even before it, but the present buildings are much later, and date from 1282. In 1492 the castle was bought by Sir Henry Wyatt, who added further buildings. His son, Thomas, was a poet of distinction who used the Italian sonnet form with great skill. The poet's son had a less happy fame for he was deeply involved in the plot to prevent Queen Mary (1553–8) from marrying Philip of Spain. The first meeting of the plotters was said to have taken place at Allington. Wyatt coerced his father-in-law, Lord Cobham, of Cooling Castle, into joining the rebellion but when the rebels reached London their march was badly bungled. Wyatt was captured and executed.

The castle then passed through the hands of several owners, and in 1905 was bought by Lord Conway. Lord Conway then spent twenty-five years and £70,000 restoring it. In 1951 it was acquired by the Carmelite Order, who have a retreat near by. But for the intervention of Lord

Take the A20 north of Maidstone and you will find a turning to Allington after 2 miles: the Tudor Garage is opposite the turning. Allington is an extremely beautiful castle and is open all the year round 2–4 p.m. It is now a Carmelite Friary. The method of visiting is by guided tour.

Conway, one of the most beautiful castles in England might have now been in ruins, but in its present hands it is very much part of the heritage of the nation.

CHILHAM

The original castle dates from the eleventh century, but the present buildings are seventeenth century. The nearby village of Chilham is also of great interest.

Chilham is 4 miles west of Canterbury, along the A28. It is owned by Viscount Massereene and Ferrard. The castle itself is not open, but the gardens, which contain a heronry, an aviary, and a large variety of plants, are open on Tuesdays, Wednesdays, Thursdays, Saturdays and Sundays 2–6 p.m. There is also a Battle of Britain museum. Tea is available, and the medieval banquets, which are held at frequent intervals, are a great attraction. For details of prices, time and menu telephone (Chilham) 022 776 561.

Deal

DEAL

As visitors will immediately note, this is a Henry VIII castle, designed to fend off possible French invaders. It was built just before 1540. It saw action during the Civil War but escaped serious slighting. In World War II it was hit by a German bomb but only partly damaged!

Deal Castle is easily found, for it is on the coast in the town itself. It is in the care of the Department of the Environment and open:
15 March–15 October, 9.30 a.m.–6.30 p.m. daily including Sunday;
16 October–14 March, 9.30 a.m.–4 p.m.
Closed Maundy Thursday, Good Friday, 24, 25, 26 December and 1 January.

DOVER

This strategic site was important for fortification from the earliest times; there are traces of earthworks of the Iron Age, there is a Roman lighthouse, and there is a church of Saxon date. Dover has seen plenty of war. William the Conqueror fought a battle here soon after Hastings and then lost a number of men from dysentery and cholera. As Dover was a Parliamentary stronghold, the castle escaped damage during the Civil War, but it was not so lucky in the eighteenth century when it was 'modified'. It was garrisoned in the Napoleonic Wars and was a military headquarters in World War II. Although this part of Kent was known as 'Hellfire Corner', owing to the amount of German bombing and shelling, Dover Castle escaped relatively unscathed. Few castles are as impressive as Dover, which looks what it is – massive and powerful.

The sight of Dover Castle on the cliff top, whether one approaches from sea or land, is not easily forgotten. It is in the care of the Department of the Environment and open:
15 March–15 October, 9.30 a.m.–6.30 p.m. daily including Sunday;
16 October–14 March, 9.30 a.m.–4 p.m.
Closed Maundy Thursday, Good Friday, 24, 25, 26 December and 1 January.

Dover

EYNSFORD

William d'Eynesford built a castle here in 1100. His son was involved in a dispute with Thomas Becket, and after the latter's murder in Canterbury Cathedral d'Eynesford was so overcome with remorse – although he had had no part in the murder – that he became a monk. (Knights often founded monasteries and sometimes became monks in them as a form of penance for past misdeeds.) After the d'Eynesfords died out in the thirteenth century, the castle was the scene of violent disputes over its ownership. After the Middle Ages it was neglected and partly demolished; however it is now properly cared for and there is much to see.

Eynsford is between Sevenoaks and Dartford off the A225. It is in the care of the Department of the Environment and open:
15 March–15 October, 9.30 a.m.–6.30 p.m. daily including Sunday;
16 October–14 March, 9.30 a.m.–4 p.m.
Closed Maundy Thursday, Good Friday, 24, 25, 26 December and 1 January.

HEVER

The castle takes its name from the Hevers or Everes who owned the manor in 1200. It was fortified by Sir John Cobham in 1380, but after him had many owners, including the Scropes, Sir John Fastolf (*see* Caister Castle) and Sir Roger Fiennes. The latter sold it to Sir Henry Boleyn (or Bullen), Lord Mayor of London in 1462. Less than a hundred years later Anne Boleyn became Henry VIII's mistress, then his wife. She was executed, as was her brother, but her daughter became Queen Elizabeth I. In 1903 Hever was bought by W. W. Astor who used a vast army of workmen to restore it and lay out the gardens. Inside and outside it is one of the most impressive castles in the country.

Hever is 3 miles south-east of Edenbridge, on the B2026. It is owned by Lord Astor of Hever and open: 30 March–28 September on Tuesdays, Wednesdays, Fridays (but not Good Friday), Sundays and Bank Holidays 1.30–7 p.m., but the entrance gates close at 6.15 p.m. On Tuesday and Friday it closes at 6 p.m. and the last entry is at 5.15 p.m.

Leeds

LEEDS

This is said to be the most beautiful castle and setting in the world. It stands in a lake (with black swans on it). There is no connection with Leeds in Yorkshire; this one takes its name from Led, an Anglo-Saxon who fortified the site in 857. It was often in royal possession. Edward I had a bath-house (rather dark and gloomy) which is now more suitably used as a boathouse. In 1321 Leeds was the scene of a spirited siege after which fourteen people were executed.

It was restored at vast expense by the Hon Lady Baillie in this century and left as a Medical Trust. However, it is open to the public as above. Everything about this castle is magnificent: the buildings, the setting, the furniture and the paintings.

6 miles south-east of Maidstone on the B2163 (leads to Sutton Valence). Opening hours are liable to change when the castle is required for special functions. Otherwise, open daily 1 April–31 October, 1–5 p.m. Tuesdays, Wednesdays, Thursdays, Sundays and Bank Holiday Mondays. Daily in August. Lunch and tea available.

RICHBOROUGH

It is a Roman fort, not a medieval castle, and dates from the third century. The site was once on an island, for the Isle of Thanet at that time was separated from the mainland of Kent by the waters of the Wantsum.

In spite of its age it is in a fine state of preservation. The walls are 30 feet high, and the ditches look as formidable as ever. There is an excellent museum which contains an extraordinary variety of exhibits dug up on the site; they include spoons, rings, lamps, statuettes, pins, tools and weapons.

Richborough lies 1½ miles north of Sandwich, off the A256. It is in the care of the Department of the Environment, and open:
15 March–15 October, 9.30 a.m.–6.30 p.m. daily including Sunday;
16 October–14 March, 9.30 a.m.–4 p.m.
Closed Maundy Thursday, Good Friday, 24, 25, 26 December and 1 January.

ROCHESTER

A castle was built here soon after the Norman Conquest, but the great keep which may be seen today was built by Henry I in 1126. Its walls are 12 feet thick and 113 feet high; the turrets reach 125 feet. A cross-wall divides the interior into equal sections. The entrance is on the second floor.

Rochester Castle was constantly in action. In 1088 it was held by the barons against William Rufus,

Rochester Castle is easily found; it is close to Rochester Bridge. It is in the care of the Department of the Environment, and open:
15 March–15 October, 9.30 a.m.–6.30 p.m. daily including Sunday;
16 October–14 March, 9.30 a.m.–4 p.m.

Rochester

but a plague of flies of unprecedented size and fierceness caused the rebels to surrender quickly. In 1215 it stood a five-month siege against King John, and eventually fell because a long underground mine penetrated below the keep. In a hollowed-out space the miners then burnt brushwood and 'forty fat pigs, not of the better sort'. The heat from the burning fat cracked the stonework and brought down the corner tower. (It was replaced by the round one which may be seen today.) However, only after starvation and bitter fighting did the castle fall.

Rochester Castle was attacked again in 1264 by rebels against Henry III, and again in the Peasants' Revolt of 1381, but it escaped damage in the Civil War.

Closed Maundy Thursday, Good Friday, 24, 25, 26 December and 1 January.

SALTWOOD

Saltwood is one of the most beautiful castles in England, for it is very well preserved and the grounds have been made into gardens. There is also a place where children may play while the castle itself is visited.

The castle was built in the twelfth century by Henry de Essex, and had many subsequent owners. It was given to Henry VIII by Archbishop Cranmer, then Archbishop of Canterbury. Centuries before it had afforded shelter for a night to the four murderers of an earlier Archbishop of Canterbury – Thomas Becket.

Saltwood Castle is 2 miles north-east of Hythe. From the A20 take the turn south to Saltwood. It is owned by the Hon Alan Clark, and is open to the public on Sundays and Bank Holidays 25 May–27 July, 2–5.30 p.m. Open daily August except Saturdays and Mondays (excepting Bank Holiday Monday) 2–5.30 p.m. Private parties will be admitted on other days if booked in advance.
Teas available.

SISSINGHURST

The term castle is in a sense misleading because there are few fortifications. Built in Tudor times, when more comfortable houses were replacing the fortified manors of the Middle Ages, it acquired the title castle in the mid-eighteenth century when French prisoners of war were detained there. The castle was bought, in a dilapidated state, by Victoria Sackville-West and Harold Nicolson, who restored the building which had fallen into disrepair. Between them they created one of the loveliest gardens in England.

Sissinghurst Castle is 2 miles north-east of Cranbrook and 1 mile east of Sissinghurst village. It is open from Good Friday to 15 October Monday–Friday, 12 noon–6.30 p.m. and on Saturdays, Sundays and Bank Holiday Mondays 10 a.m.–6.30 p.m.
Tea is available at weekends in April, and daily from May to September.
Dogs are not admitted.

UPNOR

Upnor is an unusual castle, for it was built between 1559 and 1567 to protect the ships of Queen Elizabeth I's navy. Any sailing-ship under repair in port up a river was virtually helpless against a surprise raid; the aim of Upnor was to intercept such raiders. There were also, then and later, valuable stores at Chatham which might be burnt.

In the Civil War Upnor was in Parliamentary hands, apart from a short period when it was captured by the Royalists. However, the castle was constantly falling into disrepair. In 1667 it failed to prevent a serious Dutch raid up the Medway; its defenders had plenty of courage but insufficient ammunition. The disgrace of the Dutch raid caused further defences to be built in the area.

In the courtyard of the castle are two oak trees grown from acorns brought back from the Crimea in 1856 after the end of the Crimean War.

Upnor Castle is not easy to find, but is well worth the effort necessary. Take the A228 out of Rochester and turn off in Frindsbury by the signpost to Upnor Castle. Proceed for 2 miles. On reaching Upnor, which is a small town of considerable character, turn left into the High Street. The castle is at the water's edge. It is in the care of the Department of the Environment and open: 15 March–15 October, 9.30 a.m.–6.30 p.m. daily including Sunday; 16 October–14 March, 9.30 a.m.–4 p.m. Closed Maundy Thursday, Good Friday, 24, 25, 26 December and 1 January.

WALMER

Walmer Castle is the official residence of the Lord Warden of the Cinque Ports and contains relics of many famous Wardens. In consequence, the Henry VIII castle is in excellent repair and has palatial interiors and excellent gardens. One famous Warden was the Duke of Wellington and the castle contains many of his possessions. Here you may see the original Wellington boots, the armchair in which he died and his uncomfortable bed. Here also are his death-mask, his tea and coffee sets, his clothes and his telescope. His bed is so narrow that a friend once asked him why he slept on a mattress too narrow for him to turn over. 'When it is time to turn over it is time to turn out,' he replied.

Walmer Castle is on the coast overlooking the place where Caesar is said to have landed in 55 BC. It is in the care of the Department of the Environment and open: 15 March–15 October, 9.30 a.m.–6.30 p.m. daily including Sunday; 16 October–14 March, 9.30 a.m.–4 p.m. Closed Maundy Thursday, Good Friday, 24, 25, 26 December and 1 January.

LANCASHIRE

Lancashire is aptly described as a great industrial region but it has some attractive scenery nevertheless. Lancashire people are forthright and whole-hearted, and sociable in the extreme (particularly at Blackpool). The damp climate makes the area suitable for cotton-spinning, but in spite of the rain they play good cricket there. Lancastrians have a robust sense of humour and make up many jokes about themselves. The 'Red Rose' is the emblem of this loyal county, who think of, and drink toasts to, the Queen as Duke of Lancaster. (The Queen holds two other unusual titles. She is Lord of Man, in the Isle of Man, and Duke of Normandy in the Channel Islands.)

LANCASTER

Lancaster was in an important strategic position, for it controlled the route between the Pennines and the sea. Roger de Poitou built the great keep in 1094, but John of Gaunt built the gatehouse. The castle was held by Parliament during the Civil War and was frequently attacked, but never captured, by Royalists. It was slighted subsequently as it offered too strong a point to be occupied by rebels or invading Scots. Its function as a law court and prison is, of course, in the Norman tradition.

Blood is said to ooze from the torture chamber walls; certainly a red liquid does and people do not find it amusing when they see and touch it.

The castle is on Castle Hill in the town. As it is partly occupied by a courthouse in which important trials are held, access is naturally limited. However, it is usually open to visitors in August and at the end of April and May 10.30 a.m.–noon and 2–4 p.m. Guided tours are taken every half-hour.

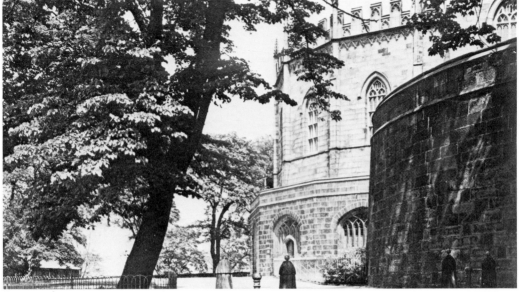

Lancaster

overleaf—Belvoir

LEICESTERSHIRE

Although Leicester is an important manufacturing town the fame of the county comes more from its fox-hunting tradition, for the large fields and high hedges demand good horses and good riders on them. Leicestershire people are proud of the Quorn Hunt and many follow on foot. The most celebrated master of the Quorn was Squire Osbaldeston, who had gambled away a fortune by his thirties. Loughborough is the centre of other forms of sport – mainly athletics, as well as a university town. Rutland has now been united with Leicestershire and the former name only persists in Rutland Water, an artificial lake.

ASHBY-DE-LA-ZOUCH

Ashby Castle began its tumultuous life as a hunting-lodge for Hugh de Grentmeisnel, who held huge tracts of land in Leicestershire in the eleventh century, but it did not acquire its full name until it became a possession of the de la Zouch family in the twelfth century. (Zouch is in Brittany.) Alan de la Zouch built part of it in stone, but the main Zouch family died out in 1314. In 1460 Ashby belonged to the Earl of Ormonde, but he fought on the losing side in the battle of Towton, Yorkshire, and was beheaded. His lands were given to Lord Hastings, who met a similar fate twenty-two years later (*see* Kirby Muxloe Castle).

The Hastings family managed to retain Ashby and during the Civil War Colonel Hastings held it for the king. He further strengthened the castle and dug two underground passages, one of which a visitor may walk through still. Ashby put up a tremendous fight before it fell in 1646, but this was ultimately to its detriment for subsequently the Parliamentarians saw that it was well slighted. Ashby was the scene of the tournament in Sir Walter Scott's *Ivanhoe*.

The Castle is easy to find as it is close to the centre of the town. It is in the care of the Department of the Environment, and open:
15 March–15 October, 9.30 a.m.–6.30 p.m. daily including Sunday;
16 October–14 March, 9.30 a.m.–4 p.m.
Closed Maundy Thursday, Good Friday, 24, 25, 26 December and 1 January.

BELVOIR

The first castle was built by Robert Todeni soon after the Norman Conquest; at that time it was known as Belvedere. It went to the Ros family who adventured recklessly, but not always skilfully, in the wars of the Middle Ages; one was hanged by Edward IV. Lord Hastings acquired Belvoir and

Belvoir is 7 miles south-west of Grantham, off the A607. Opening times are:
26 March–28 September, Wednesdays, Thursdays, Fridays 12–6 p.m.; Sundays 2–7 p.m. In October it is

removed some of the stone to build Ashby-de-la-Zouch Castle. Belvoir was rebuilt in the sixteenth century but slighted after the Civil War. It was finally rebuilt as a mansion by the Duke of Rutland in 1800 and now contains magnificent pictures and furniture, as well as the museum of the 17/21st Lancers.

open on Sundays 2–6 p.m. It is also open on Bank Holidays.
Food and tea may be obtained at the castle. The telephone number is (Knipton) 047 682 262, for those who wish to check that there has been no change in opening times.

KIRBY MUXLOE

The Hastings family had held a manor here since the thirteenth century, but the present castle was begun by Lord Hastings, who was summarily, and possibly unjustly, beheaded by Richard III in 1483. The scene is well-known to those who have seen or read Shakespeare's *Richard III*. Lord Hastings was extremely wealthy and built the tower at Ashby-de-la-Zouch. However, he partly demolished Belvoir for the materials.

Kirby Muxloe is a most interesting castle for two principal reasons. One is that it was designed for the age of gunpowder, although the site suggests that Hastings failed to appreciate how quickly range would increase. Secondly, the building accounts are almost complete. The master-mason had also built Eton and Winchester colleges. A Dutchman was in charge of the brick-kiln where they manufactured 100,000 bricks a week. Most of the other craftsmen were Welsh. Judging by their lasting qualities, there was nothing wrong with the manufacture of medieval bricks.

Four miles west of Leicester, in an unobtrusive position, a brick castle which was never finished. It lies midway between the A47 and the A50. It is in the care of the Department of the Environment and open:
15 March–15 October, 9.30 a.m.–6.30 p.m. daily including Sunday;
16 October–14 March, 9.30 a.m.–4 p.m.
Closed Maundy Thursday, Good Friday, 24, 25, 26 December and 1 January.

OAKHAM

Only the great hall and a few earthworks remain of the castle built by Earl Ferrers. Many of its owners met violent deaths, one was killed at Agincourt in 1415.

Earl Ferrers was a royal farrier and had the right to stop peers who visited the town or passed through for the first time and ask for a horseshoe. This was then returned, on payment of a sum of money, and a horseshoe showing the size of the money paid over was fixed on the wall. Most of the original horseshoes rusted away but the modern versions are interesting.

In the town.
Open daily, April–September, 9.30 a.m.–8.30 p.m.; October–March, 9.30 a.m.–4 p.m.

LINCOLNSHIRE

Lincolnshire is a huge county, even though it has now lost a piece of its northern territory to help make Humberside. Lincolnshire has the famous Wolds (downs) and some of the finest agricultural land in the country. Lincoln still bears signs of having been a Roman town, and the cathedral is not to be missed. King John lost his treasure when travelling through the country and caught by flood water; it is somewhere near the Wash but the chances of it ever being discovered again are not rated highly.

LINCOLN

Lincoln was originally a fortified Roman town. The first castle was begun in 1068 and it is still possible – though arduous – to ascend the old motte. The cathedral stands in what was formerly the bailey.

Lincoln has seen a lot of fighting: in the anarchy of Stephen, in the wars of King John and Henry III, and in the Civil War when it was captured by the Parliamentarians. The building extends over $6\frac{1}{4}$ acres, and like Lewes has the rare feature of a double motte.

Cobb Hall in the north-east angle of the curtain wall was where the executions were carried out. It was used until 1859, after which executions took place inside the castle until 1877. The dungeon, the iron rings to which prisoners were chained, the gloom, are all evident today.

The castle is in the centre of the city and is open to the public from April to September 10 a.m.–4 p.m. and from October to March 2–4 p.m. The Assize Courts, when not in session, are not open to the public, but it is possible to ascend the walls and towers and even descend into the former condemned cell.

Lincoln

TATTERSHALL

There was an earlier castle on this site but the present one, which now consists of an enormous brick tower, was built by Lord Ralph Cromwell, who was Treasurer of England 1433–43. Subsequently it had many owners but eventually became uninhabited, and neglected, for two hundred years. In 1910 the ruin was bought by an American firm of speculators. The fireplaces had already been sent to London, en route for America, when Lord Curzon stepped in, repurchased the castle and fireplaces, and had the castle restored (compare Bodiam). When the restoration was complete, Lord Curzon bequeathed the castle to the National Trust. Today it is possible to walk from floor to floor and finally look over the battlements which are 100 feet high. Until you see Tattershall you will not really believe any castle could be like this and in such fine condition.

Tattershall is 12 miles from Sleaford, on the A153. It is owned by the National Trust and is open daily 11 a.m.–6.30 p.m., and on Sundays 1–6.30 p.m., or sunset, whichever is the earlier. From 1 October to 31 March the castle is closed on weekdays 1–2 p.m.

Tattershall

LONDON

Of London's castles, two have disappeared, as have all the city gates, except in name. However the Tower of London, or White Tower as the original building is called, is enough to fulfil anyone's dream of a castle. Baynard's Castle was on the Thames, near St Paul's; part of the foundations were found in rebuilding work recently. Montfichet was on Addle Hill, E.C.4, and Ravenger's Castle is known to have existed but nobody is sure where.

THE TOWER OF LONDON

The White Tower is the Norman keep which was built by William the Conqueror, starting, it is believed, in 1076. It is part of the concentric castle which is the Tower of London.

The White Tower is so called because it was painted white (compare Conwy, Whitecastle etc). The White Tower is 90 feet high and has an almost continental look but, apart from some windows which were altered by Sir Christopher Wren, its appearance has changed very little from the original.

Its military strength, with its 100 feet moats and its flanking towers, is immediately obvious. It is still garrisoned, and in World War II it was bombed. Its association with British history is interesting but macabre. Here are the Traitor's Gate, the Bloody Tower, the staircase where the children's bones (perhaps those of the murdered princes) were found, and Raleigh's Walk; few places are so evocative and sinister. This was the first Norman stone castle.

The nearest Underground station is Tower Hill.
The Tower is in the care of the Department of the Environment and open:
15 March–15 October, 9.30 a.m.–6.30 p.m. daily including Sunday;
16 October–14 March, 9.30 a.m.–4 p.m.
The Tower of London is closed on Sundays from early October to early March, but the Sunday service in the Chapel of St Peter ad Vincula is open to the public.
Closed Maundy Thursday, Good Friday, 24, 25, 26 December.and 1 January.

Tower of London

NORFOLK

When the Angles came to what became East Anglia (before they gave their name to the whole country as Angle-land), they settled in two groups, as the North Folk and the South Folk. This area was formerly separate from the rest of Britain, isolated by fens and protected by ramparts. Later this changed completely; Norwich became a centre for the wool trade and weaving, and King's Lynn became a busy port; the northern coast and the Broads became favourite holiday places.

Norfolk has a number of country houses: Felbrigg, Blickling, Holkham, Houghton, and, of course, Sandringham. Oxburgh Hall, although a late fifteenth-century manor house, is more of a castle than many which bear the name. The 80 feet great tower and the wide moat would have given a would-be attacker reason to pause. Oxburgh is open from April until October every afternoon, 2–6 p.m., except on Fridays and Mondays (but open on Bank Holiday Mondays). The Bedingfield family have lived here since it was built. Oxburgh is 7 miles south-west of Swaffham.

BACONSTHORPE

Although a ruin, it has many interesting and puzzling features. It was built in the period 1450–70 by the Heydon family. The design is puzzling because the building does not conform to the pattern one would expect in a fifteenth-century castle, but this may be because much of the masonry has been removed for building elsewhere (sold, in fact, by a seventeenth-century owner who fell on hard times). The castle's military capabilities were never put to the test, but it is of interest because it belonged to the latest phase of medieval castle development and might well have been a formidable problem for an attacker.

Baconsthorpe Castle is approached by the A148 from King's Lynn to Cromer; it is 3 miles east of Holt and ¾ mile north of Baconsthorpe village. It is in the care of the Department of the Environment and open:
15 March–15 October, 9.30 a.m.–6.30 p.m. daily including Sunday;
16 October–14 March, 9.30 a.m.–4 p.m.
Closed Maundy Thursday, Good Friday, 24, 25, 26 December and 1 January.

Baconsthorpe

CAISTER

Caister is a brick castle which was built from ransom-money after Sir John Fastolf (who became Shakespeare's Falstaff) captured a French knight at Agincourt (1415). On Fastolf's death it went to the Pastons who had to fight the Duke of Norfolk to retain its possession – with thirty against three thousand. They lost, but regained the castle later. Margaret Paston, an exceptional woman, wrote a series of letters to her husband from which we obtain a clear idea of what life was like in the fifteenth century. They, and others by members of the family, were later published as *The Paston Letters*.

Caister Castle is 3 miles north of Yarmouth, just off the A1064. It is owned by Mr P. R. Hill who has maintained it and made it very entertaining for the visitor. It is open from May to September, 10.30 a.m.– 5 p.m.
On the premises there is a motor museum which will interest even those who are indifferent to cars.

CASTLE ACRE

Recent excavations have disclosed some of the complexities of this large and powerful castle built by William de Warenne, 1st Earl of Surrey. The Warennes were a turbulent family who were immensely powerful before the legitimate line died out in 1347, and the priory they founded here was far from being a centre of holiness and asceticism.

Buckenham, three miles south-west of Attleborough, has the earthworks of a castle built in 1136 which is similar in plan to Castle Acre. Little of it remains.

Four miles north of Swaffham is Castle Acre, and near by is the Priory. Both are in the care of the Department of the Environment, but the former is open at all times. Originally the priory was inside the bailey of the castle.

CASTLE RISING

Originally Castle Rising was on the sea, but the topography here has changed. The Norman keep, which is still impressive today, was built by William d'Albini, 'The Strong Hand', who is supposed to have pulled out a lion's tongue. At one time the mighty Warenne family held Castle Rising. Queen Isabella, 'She-Wolf of France', who connived at the murder of her husband, Edward II (*see* Berkeley Castle), was imprisoned here for thirty years by her son Edward III. 'Imprisoned' probably meant no more than 'was made to live here'. An impressive castle inside huge earthworks.

Castle Rising is easily found, just off the A149 4 miles north of King's Lynn. It is in the care of the Department of the Environment and open:
15 March–15 October, 9.30 a.m.–6.30 p.m. daily including Sunday;
16 October–14 March, 9.30 a.m.–4 p.m.
Closed Maundy Thursday, Good Friday, 24, 25, 26 December and 1 January.

NORWICH

Norwich Castle, which still occupies a dominant
site, once spread over a much larger area – the size
of the keep alone gives the visitor a good insight
into what the castle must have been like. Norwich
has made excellent use of its historic past. Whereas
certain other towns have been content to allow
their castles to become a ruin in a public park,
Norwich has established four museums – one in
the keep itself – and a rotunda where the visitor
may sit and have tea, look at exhibits, or merely
ponder. Exceptional imagination and good sense
have been used and the museum has rooms
showing birds, mammals and other inhabitants of
the Norfolk countryside, besides pottery, glass,
silver and paintings amidst much of interest.

In the city and owned by it.
Open on weekdays 10 a.m.–
5 p.m. and Sundays 2.30–
5 p.m.

The first castle was built in 1067, destroying a
hundred houses in the process, but the present
building dates from 1125. The keep was faced with
Caen stone, brought from Normandy. It was easy
to work, but hardened like granite. The keep is 76
feet high and 96 feet by 76 feet in area. The
castle's early holders were turbulent and often in
trouble. In 1549, when Robert Kett's rebellion had
been defeated at nearby Mousehold Heath, Kett
was hanged from the battlements. His peasant
followers were treated with great harshness, but
Norwich is proud of Kett today.

THETFORD

Thetford has the distinction of being the largest
motte and bailey castle in England. Its vast size is
due to its being constructed on an Iron Age fort.
The fortified part of it was destroyed in 1174 by
Henry II when he was curbing the power of the
barons. It looks impregnable, but . . .

In the town of Thetford.

NORTHAMPTONSHIRE

Northampton has a long-standing reputation as a centre for fine footwear but the county has other attractions too. It is a good agricultural district and is the home of the Pytchley Hunt. Among the many famous stately homes are: Castle Ashby (an Elizabethan mansion), Althorp, Boughton House, Deene Park, and Sulgrave Manor (where George Washington's family lived). There are few castles, although Rockingham, described below, is of exceptional interest. Barnwell Castle, near Oundle, is twelfth century but is in the grounds of the home of H.R.H. the Duke of Gloucester. It is, however, occasionally open to the public under the National Gardens Scheme and dates and times may be found in the local Press. Fotheringay, of which only one wall remains, was the birthplace of Richard III and the place where Mary, Queen of Scots, was executed. It was demolished in 1645 and some of the stone was taken to build the Talbot Hotel in Oundle. There is a motte at Lilbourne, and there are a few remains at Earl's Barton, Rushton and Thorpe Waterville. The really sad story is the fate of the once powerful Northampton castle, which was completely demolished to make room for a railway station and yards. Railway building was extremely destructive of castles, much more so than modern motorways have been.

ROCKINGHAM

The first castle was built by William the Conqueror but the present castle is the result of rebuilding in the sixteenth century. It was badly damaged by the Roundheads in the Civil War, but has since been extremely well cared for. The massive drum towers are thirteenth century (compare Chirk); inside are many attractive rooms and much superb furniture and china. Charles Dickens produced and acted in several plays in the Gallery. He also saw a ghost here.

14 miles from Stamford on the A427. 2 miles north of Corby, 9 miles from Market Harborough. Open: Easter Sunday–30 September, Sundays and Thursdays and Bank Holiday Mondays and Tuesdays 2–4 p.m. Tea available.

Rockingham

NORTHUMBERLAND

The most northerly county of England is unknown to many, but is full of interest. Its scenery is varied and beautiful and history is everywhere. Hadrian's Wall, which stretches from Solway Firth in the west to Tynemouth in the east (73 miles), is mostly in Northumberland. Every few miles along it was a formidable fortress, a miniature castle. The average height of the wall was 15 feet and it was never less than 7 feet thick. There are battlefields here: at Hexham; at Halidon Hill; at Otterburn, where in 1388 the Scots trounced the English, and at Flodden, where in 1513 the English destroyed the Scottish army. There is, sadly, no castle at Berwick, a town which has seen more battles than most, but there are still earth ramparts. Berwick, even without its former castle and latterly much despoiled by town-planners, is still richly rewarding to visit. Near by is Coldstream, the small village whose name was adopted by what has become one of the most famous regiments of the British army, the Coldstream Guards. Here too is Holy Island, but the castle, though interesting, is not a true medieval one. These border counties, the marches, were great reserves of fighting men for both English and Scots, if not fighting each other, which was often enough, were fighting among themselves, and sometimes doing both at the same time.

ALNWICK

The first castle at Alnwick was probably built in 1140 but the present building is the result of much extension and restoration. It is a most rewarding castle to visit, for the visitor feels both welcome and understood. Alnwick is the home of the Duke of Northumberland, so it is a lived-in castle. The attractive town of Alnwick, where you may eat and stay, is also the home of the world-famous makers

Alnwick, pronounced 'Annick', is just off the A1, 30 miles north of Newcastle. It takes its name from the River Alne. The castle is open daily, except Saturdays, 1–5 p.m., May to October.
No dogs.

Alnwick

of fly-fishing equipment, Hardy of Alnwick. If there is a fisherman in the party you may have trouble with him here if you have a full itinerary.

Alnwick has probably seen more action than most castles, partly because of its situation close to the Scottish border, and partly because of the great fighting qualities of its holders. The first of these were the De Vescey family, whose last surviving male was killed at Bannockburn in 1314, the second were the Percy family. A Percy had come over to England in 1066 with William the Conqueror, and even before coming to Alnwick the family was renowned for its fighting qualities. In the early days the title was Lord Percy of Alnwick, but in 1377 this became Earl. The male line and title became extinct in 1670, but a daughter continued the line and in 1766 the husband of the female descendant was granted the title of Duke.

During the Middle Ages the Percy family waged an almost continuous but not unchivalrous war with the Douglas family from over the border. One of their battles is commemorated in the 'Ballad of Chevy Chase'. Earl after earl died a violent death in battle, as did many of their near relations. Typical was the 4th Earl who died at the age of sixty-seven in a night battle (resulting from an irresponsible rebellion) and his son who gained battle honours at the siege of Berwick when only twelve years old.

Much of Alnwick has been restored, and it is not easy to know which parts are very old. Most of the stone figures on the roof are eighteenth century, but a few date from the fourteenth. They were deception targets for enemy archers to waste their arrows on.

BAMBURGH

The site was fortified in Roman times, but the castle dates from the Norman period and was the scene of a rebellion against William Rufus. Henry II and Henry III built extensively, the former being responsible for the massive keep. It had enormous strategic value as a strong-point close to the invasion route from Scotland. One of its more notable commanders was Harry Percy (Hotspur) who won the battle of Homildon Hill against the Scots. He was somewhat misrepresented by

Bamburgh is 16 miles north of Alnwick, 50 miles north of Newcastle, and 70 miles south of Edinburgh. From April to the end of October it is open every day 1–7.30 p.m., when visitors are taken on conducted tours.

Shakespeare.

During the Wars of the Roses it had the dubious distinction of being the first castle in England to fall to gunfire – but mainly through poor morale (1464).

Lord Armstrong restored the castle in 1894, and it now contains eleven flats, and houses more people than at any time since the Middle Ages. Although much added to since medieval times, Bamburgh is exactly what one expects a powerful medieval castle to look like, and its story is rich in unusual history. Bamburgh township is a pleasant place in which to stay.

DUNSTANBURGH

Dunstanburgh was an enormous castle on a remote coastal site covering ten acres. It should have been impregnable but did not prove to be so. It was begun by the Earl of Lancaster, resolute opponent of Edward II; Lancaster decided he might at some time require a secure retreat, so built a keep 80 feet high and a moat 80 feet wide. However, he was unable to use it for he was ignominiously executed in Pontefract after losing the Battle of Boroughbridge in 1322. The castle was later added to by John of Gaunt, but in the Wars of the Roses it capitulated very rapidly to gunfire. Yet, few castles match its splendour in ruins.

The castle lies 1½ miles from Craster, and whichever way you approach it involves a stimulating walk. Visitors with cars are advised to park them as near as possible, otherwise the walk becomes unduly lengthy. The castle is in the care of the Department of the Environment, and open:
15 March–15 October, 9.30 a.m.–6.30 p.m. daily including Sunday;
16 October–14 March, 9.30 a.m.–4 p.m.
Closed Maundy Thursday, Good Friday, 24, 25, 26 December and 1 January.

NORHAM

Norham is a veritable symbol of strength, with a massive keep 90 feet high and 60 feet by 84 feet in area, but that did not mean it was unchallenged. An earlier castle, built in 1121, was destroyed by the Scots; the present building dates from 1174. Although, theoretically, it belonged to the Bishops of Durham, it often returned to royal ownership. In 1215 it withstood a forty-day siege by the Scots. In 1318, 1319 and 1322 it beat off other sieges but

Norham is 8 miles south-west of Berwick and 7 miles north-east of Coldstream. It is on the east of the village, on the bank of the Tweed. It is in the care of the Department of the Environment, and open:
15 March–15 October, 9.30 a.m.–6.30 p.m. daily including Sunday;

in 1327 it fell. It was involved in the Wars of the Roses, and again in war with Scotland in the sixteenth century. However, it escaped involvement in the Civil War.

In its heyday this magnificent castle was where, to use a modern idiom, 'it all happened'. Any young knight or squire wishing to prove his mettle had only to post himself to Norham, where he would find hard knocks, sharp swords, and critical or approving eyes and, if he proved himself, acceptance. Norham was a front-line castle and those who fought there gained prestige in the eyes of fellow-men – and fellow-women.

16 October–14 March, 9.30 a.m.– 4 p.m.
Closed Maundy Thursday, Good Friday, 24, 25, 26 December and 1 January.

WARKWORTH

The present buildings date from the twelfth and thirteenth centuries although the site had been fortified earlier. It was the property of the powerful Percy family and still is. The Duke of Northumberland occasionally stays here, in the keep, but the rest of the castle is a ruin, although an attractive one.

Warkworth has stood several sieges. It also figures in Shakespeare's *Henry IV, Part I*. In the Civil War it was captured by the Scots (1644), was given up in 1645, re-occupied by Parliament in 1648, but badly damaged at their withdrawal. The greatest damage to it was done in 1672 when it was pillaged for building materials, but much still remains for the visitor to see, and it is quite impressive.

Warkworth is 6 miles south-east of Alnwick in a horse-shoe bend of the River Coquet. It is in the care of the Department of the Environment, and open:
15 March–15 October, 9.30 a.m.–6.30 p.m. daily including Sunday;
16 October–14 March, 9.30 a.m.–4 p.m.
Closed Maundy Thursday, Good Friday, 24, 25, 26 December and 1 January.

Warkworth

NOTTINGHAMSHIRE

Nottinghamshire is famed for Sherwood Forest and the legendary activities of Robin Hood and his band of merry men. Robin Hoods have been reported from many areas but not all have been as chivalrous and benevolent as Robin Hood of Nottingham. Robin Hood of Nottingham and Sherwood Forest is said to have flourished in the reign of Richard I (1189–99) who spent only eight months of his ten year rule in his kingdom but had a natural authority which kept his barons, if not his outlaws, in order. An outlaw, in medieval times, was a criminal who had been banished from a district or, if still living there, had lost all his legal rights.

NEWARK

The first castle was built by the Bishop of Lincoln in 1123, but in its history it frequently became a royal castle. King John died here in 1216, as every schoolboy knows, after losing all his treasure in the Wash and eating too many ripe peaches or, according to some accounts, lampreys. Newark's great days were in the Civil War when the Royalists held it; their earthworks, called 'sconces', may still be seen. The castle was slighted after the siege, but the remains have been well maintained since. The gatehouse, one of the largest in the country, is exceptionally impressive. During the siege the castle contained a mint, and specimen coins may be seen in the museum.

Newark Castle – what remains of it – is in the middle of the town, and is open to the public daily. Unfortunately, only one side of the castle is still standing (as viewed over the bridge), and this represents most of what is left. However, Newark is rich in history, is the site of a formidable battle in the Civil War, and has an interesting museum.

NOTTINGHAM

There is, unfortunately, not much left of this once vast castle which was begun in 1068 by William the Conqueror, 'who filled the land with castles'. Most of the building was completed in the thirteenth century. It saw little action until the Civil War – which began when Charles I raised his standard in Nottingham in 1642 – and after the war was very thoroughly dismantled.

There is a passage called 'Mortimer's Hole' by which the murderer of Edward II, and paramour of his Queen Isabella, was captured in the castle. He was caught by surprise and executed later at Tyburn.

There is an excellent museum here which includes mementoes of Albert Ball, VC.

Nottingham Castle is on a huge sandstone cliff on the outskirts of the town. It is owned by the Nottingham corporation and is open on weekdays in the summer 10 a.m.–6.45 p.m. (5.45 p.m. on Fridays) and on Sundays 2–4.45 p.m. It is open until dusk in winter.

overleaf—Newark

OXFORDSHIRE

The centre of Oxfordshire, in several senses of the word, is Oxford. Here a walk around the colleges gives a remarkable insight into medieval life. Students originally wore gowns to keep them warm in the cold, draughty, buildings. Oxford became a royalist headquarters in the Civil War and the earthworks from this time are still visible. William Morris, the motor magnate who became Lord Nuffield, although a generous benefactor to Oxford, almost ruined it with his motor industry, so that the 'city of dreaming spires' became the 'city of screaming tyres'. The Oxfordshire countryside, from Henley-on-Thames to Banbury, is serenely beautiful without being awe-inspiring. Oxford Castle (in the town) only exists as a mound and a tower and both are in the precincts of the prison, though easy to see from the road. Bampton, Banbury, Deddington (a massive earthwork), Middleton Stoney, and Radcot had castles but they have disappeared except for traces. Minster Lovell was more of a manor than a castle but its ruins, on the A40 near Witney, are well worth a visit. Lord Lovell, having rebelled unsuccessfully against Henry VII, returned to hide here in 1487; his skeleton was found sitting at a table in a locked vault in 1708. Doubtless he had starved to death waiting for the helper who never came back. An equally macabre Lovell story is attached to Greys Court, near Henley-on-Thames. This is the mistletoe-bough legend of the bride who mistakenly hid in an old oak chest with a spring lid. She was discovered years later

> A fair young form lay mouldering there
> The bridal wreath still twined in her hair.

Greys Court also served as the prison for the murderers of Sir Thomas Overbury who was poisoned by chocolates sent as a gift.

But these are nothing compared to Blenheim Palace, at Woodstock. Blenheim is not a castle but it commemorates a family which produced the 1st Duke of Marlborough and Sir Winston Churchill.

BROUGHTON

The castle was begun in 1301 and the gatehouse and parts of the present building show its early origins; however, much of it is in the form of an Elizabethan mansion.

Broughton is strikingly beautiful at anytime of the year, but its wide moat made it highly defensible as well. In the seventeenth century Lord Saye and Sele was a keen Parliamentary supporter, and although the castle was occupied by Royalists it escaped damage. Lord Saye and Sele disapproved of the execution of Charles I and in 1660 swore loyalty to Charles II.

The original medieval hall (54 feet by 30 feet) is still preserved. This is everyone's dream of a castle.

Broughton lies 2½ miles west of Banbury on the B4035 and is the home of Lord Saye and Sele. It is open to the public June–14 September on Wednesdays and Sundays 2–5 p.m. July and August: Wednesdays, Thursdays, and Sundays 2–5 p.m. It is also open on Bank Holidays 2–5 p.m.

SHROPSHIRE

The western flank of Shropshire lies along the border of North Wales, and, in consequence, is full of remains of fortifications from Roman times onward. There are Iron Age forts, Roman garrison towns and forts, notably Uricon (Wroxeter), and medieval castles, large and small. The Normans loved fighting and the Welsh were only too ready to give them all the practice they needed. Many of the Norman castles are now only earthworks with a few fragments of masonry: Alderbury, Apley, Broncroft, Charlton, Ellesmere, Holgate, Hopton, Knockin, Myddle, Oswestry, Redcastle, Rowton and Royton are some of them. Caus, ten miles west of Shrewsbury, was named after Caux in France, and must have been very strong though not strong enough to escape destruction in the Civil War. Clun has three baileys and some unsafe masonry; this was indeed a front-line castle. Whittington, two miles east of Oswestry, still has an impressive gatehouse and towers which the A5 passes. These remains in a peaceful countryside are a sharp reminder that at times Shropshire was more like an armed camp than a quiet agricultural county. The county name was changed to Salop in 1974 but local feeling (and pressure) had the earlier name restored in 1980.

ACTON BURNELL

There is a substantial quantity of masonry to see here, and it is all beautifully kept. The castle's days of glory were from 1284 to 1420, after which it was abandoned.

Acton Burnell is small as castles go, and this has caused it to be cited as an early example of a manor-house. Acton means 'a clearing in an oak forest'; and the surrounding woodlands were a considerable financial asset to the owner. Acton became Acton Burnell through the efforts of Roger Burnell, a clerk in the service of Edward I (1272–1307). Burnell was diligent and able, and in due course became Chancellor. From this post he was made Bishop of Bath and Wells. Edward tried to arrange that Burnell should become Archbishop of Canterbury, but Edward was no Henry VIII and was not prepared to defy the power of the Roman Catholic Church for the sake of his favourite clerk. However, Edward was able to grant Burnell this manor in Shropshire with permission to cut timber in the Royal Forests of Shropshire. The Burnells held the castle until the mid-fifteenth century, after which it had several distinguished owners: one was Henry VII, another was the Earl of Surrey, victor of Flodden.

Acton Burnell is 4 miles from Shrewsbury in the direction of Wenlock Edge. It is not difficult to find, but as you approach the vicinity you might have to ask for directions from a local inhabitant as you are likely to go astray on the minor roads. The castle is open all the time, and is free. It is looked after by the Department of the Environment.

BRIDGNORTH

Bridgnorth commands the point where the Bristol to Chester road crosses the River Severn and this was clearly of great strategic importance. It had been fortified from a very early date, perhaps pre-Roman. In 912 Aethelfaed, (Ethelfleda), the 'Lady of Mercia', otherwise described as 'that woman who was the terror of men', built a burh (fortification) here. In 1101 Robert of Belesme, Earl of Shrewsbury, built a castle on the site, from which he tried without success to defy his monarch, Henry I. Belesme already owned thirty-four castles in Normandy, and, in modern terms, was a psychopath who preferred to torture his prisoners rather than have them ransomed. After 1102 Belesme himself spent his remaining years in prison. Bridgnorth was often engaged in fighting, but the final round came in 1646 when it was attacked by Parliamentary forces and made to surrender, though partly by bluff. It was then slighted, leaving the astonishing sight of a tower leaning 17 degrees from the perpendicular. In the slighting it was lifted 3 feet but has stood ever since in its present remarkable position. Compare this with Caerphilly and Bramber.

Bridgnorth Castle, which is on top of the hill in the town, was once an immensely powerful structure, but today only a portion of wall and a bizarre leaning tower remain. It is open daily.

LUDLOW

Ludlow Castle was built at the end of the eleventh century by Roger de Lacy. It was a Marcher castle, i.e. it was to guard the marches (borders) and as such it saw plenty of fighting. When Stephen was

The castle is in the town and is open from April to September 10.30 a.m.–1 p.m. and 2 p.m. until dusk, Sundays included. In the

besieging it in 1138, a companion was snatched up by a grappling-hook but Stephen managed to unhook him. Soon after, Ludlow was betrayed by an amorous young Lady, Marion de la Bruyère, who let in her treacherous lover by rope ladder; he left the ladder hanging and a hundred armed men followed him. Ludlow was heavily involved in the Wars of the Roses and again in the Civil War. There is a lot to see here, and it is all picturesque and peaceful, but it was indeed a great fighting castle. It was also the setting in 1634 for the first performance of Milton's *Comus*.

winter, it is open 10.30 a.m. –4.30 p.m., and on Sundays by arrangement. Conducted tours are available.

SHREWSBURY

Roger of Montgomery built a wooden castle here in 1080, and until the thirteenth century most of the castle and bailey was of the same material. When the castle was besieged and captured by King Stephen, in 1138, he was so irritated by the arrogance of the garrison that he hanged ninety-three of them. This was surprising as he was normally patient and forgiving to the point of disaster – from the standpoint of the country he was supposed to be ruling. Shrewsbury was always important, for it was a key rear headquarters for campaigns in Wales. In the Civil War it was captured by Parliament in a surprise night attack. Later it fell into ruin but was restored in a ridiculous way by Thomas Telford, so that Sir William Pulteney MP 'could live in a suitable state'. Fortunately, a good portion escaped the 'improvements'.

Shrewsbury Castle is in the centre of the town and is open from March to 31 October. Visiting times are 9 p.m.–12 noon and 2–5 p.m.; Sundays 2–5 p.m.

STOKESAY

Stokesay is really a thirteenth-century fortified manor with later additions. It is astonishingly beautiful, and most visitors use up a lot of camera film here. It was surrendered to Parliamentary forces in the Civil War and the subsequent slighting was slight. The two outstanding features – among many of interest – are the Great Hall, which dates from the thirteenth century, and the seventeenth-century gatehouse.

Stokesay is just off the A49 (Shrewsbury – Ludlow). It is owned by Lady Magnus Allcroft and is open to the public daily (except Tuesdays) in summer 10 a.m.–6 p.m. and March to October 10 a.m.–5 p.m. No one is admitted half an hour before closing time. It is closed November–February inclusively.

SOMERSET

In the Dark Ages when it was at the western end of the Saxon kingdom of Wessex this was called Sumorsaete. As a county Somerset is full of surprises, not the least being a typical French medieval castle at Nunney in the heart of rural English countryside. Somerset has something for everyone: Exmoor for the walkers; a notable battlefield at Sedgemoor for the historian; Wookey Hole and the Mendips for the potholer; Avalon for the romantic; Cadbury Castle and Glastonbury for those who wish to rekindle the past, and Wells for the student of cathedral architecture. Today, Somerset seems to exude peace and goodwill but it was not always so, as its historical relics show. Judge Jeffreys held the Bloody Assizes in the Great Hall of Taunton Castle and many of his victims were executed in the streets outside. Alfred retreated to Somerset when he had been defeated and driven back by the Danes; from his hiding place he planned and launched his triumphant return.

Wells Cathedral has a 1390 clock in which figures of armed horsemen rotate, one is beaten down on each circuit; it belongs to a martial age. The Bishop's Palace from the same period is a reminder of warlike bishops and turbulent times; it is as formidable as a castle. However, swans now swim in the moat and pull on a rope when they wish to be fed.

DUNSTER

Dunster Castle has been in the possession of the Luttrell family since 1376. (There was a previous owner called William de Mohun.) The castle is now administered by the National Trust. Dunster is an excellent example of what a dedicated family can do to keep a private castle in repair, even if the effort is enormous and a great financial burden.

During the Civil War Dunster was besieged by the Parliamentarians but escaped demolition. Inside is a magnificent seventeenth-century staircase, hall and interior, and many portraits.

Dunster was once a centre for woollen cloth weaving and gave its name to a certain type of cloth. Similarly, worsted took its name from Worstead in Norfolk and jeans from Génes (Genoa).

The castle is in Dunster, which is 3 miles south-east of Minehead on the A396.
Opening times:
6 April–30 September, daily (except Fridays and Saturdays) 11 a.m.–5p.m.;
October: Tuesdays, Wednesdays and Sundays 2–4 p.m.
Last admission half hour before closing. No dogs.
Shop. Deer park and terraced gardens.
Tea at Luttrell Arms.

FARLEIGH HUNGERFORD

If ever a castle deserved to be haunted it is certainly this one. Seeing its peaceful setting one

3 miles west of Trowbridge
Open:

little realises how much doom and evil have been associated with this place.

In the eleventh century it was a manor named Farleigh Montfort but 1369 gave it a new owner, Sir Thomas de Hungerford, who changed its name. In the late fifteenth century Robert Hungerford was a prisoner of war for seven years in France but after release was executed for being on the losing side in the Wars of the Roses. Five years later his eldest son was executed. In 1523 Lady Agnes Hungerford was hanged at Tyburn for strangling her first husband and burning his body in the kitchen furnace at Farleigh. Her stepson, Walter Hungerford, married three times but imprisoned his third wife in one of the towers and gave her little food and some of it was poisoned. He himself was soon after executed by Henry VIII for Catholic sympathies and unnatural vice. (His wife married again and bore her husband six children!) The castle was confiscated but the new owner was soon executed also and the land came back to the next Hungerford.

This one charged his wife with adultery and attempted poisoning but lost his case; he tried to settle the castle on his own mistress but failed in that also. In the Civil War members of the family fought on opposite sides; one tried to marry one of Cromwell's daughters. One disaster followed another until the early 1700s when Edward 'the Spendthrift' gambled away twenty-eight manors and died in poverty; the total fortune lost was worth several million pounds at today's values. A last gamble to raise money was to turn his London house and garden into a market. This became Hungerford Market.

The lead coffins in the vaults have faces moulded on them.

15 March–15 October, 9.30 a.m.–6.30 p.m. daily including Sunday;
16 October–16 March, 9.30 a.m.–4 p.m. including Sundays.

NUNNEY

Nunney is a small, very beautiful castle in an attractive town. It was built by John de la Mare in 1373 and is essentially French in design – compare parts of Warwick castle. The outworks covered a larger area than they do today but the design was based on the defensive ideas of the pre-gunpowder era and made a poor showing against 36-pounder

Nunney is 3 miles south-west of Frome. The castle is in the care of the Department of the Environment. The key is obtainable from the caretaker's cottage (directions about this are at

cannon in the Civil War in 1645. One wall was knocked down and the castle held out for two days only against the besieging Parliamentary forces; however as the garrison consisted of a captain, eight Irishmen, and some refugees, it could not have stood up against a besieging army very effectively. Morale too was low: Royalist hopes had been extinguished when the Battle of Naseby had been lost three months earlier. The fact that the Royalist holder offered his services (which were refused) to the Parliamentarians after the surrender and that the castle was hardly slighted at all suggests that the siege was never meant to be more than a token. But with a larger garrison, stronger morale and a few modifications (including some gunports) Nunney could have been a very tough proposition indeed.

Perhaps these open-plan castles like Nunney and Bodiam were a less effective design than the tried and proved concentric and linear castles which they claimed to have outmoded (*see* Introduction).

the castle entrance) at opening times, which are:
16 October–14 March, 9.30 a.m.–4 p.m., Sundays, 2–4 p.m.;
15 March–15 October, 9.30 a.m.–6.30 p.m., Sundays 2 –6.30 p.m.
Closed Maundy Thursday, Good Friday, 24, 25, 26 December and 1 January.

TAUNTON

At the Castle Hotel, which is built on part of the site of the inner moat and the castle keep, you may obtain a useful little guide-book with an instructive map. There were earthworks on this site centuries before the Normans built a castle in 1127. It was involved in Perkin Warbeck's rebellion in 1497, was the centre of heavy fighting during the Civil War 1642–5 and was Monmouth's army headquarters in 1685. Subsequent trials by Judge Jeffreys took place here. Soon afterwards the castle was dismantled but much has been restored in the luxury Castle Hotel which has medieval remains and every modern comfort. The castle garden contains the old (rare type) square well. The site also has a museum (open 10 a.m.–4 p.m., except Sundays) and a library.

Taunton needs no directions. The castle is in St James's Street. Most of it is now part of the Taunton Castle Hotel.

STAFFORDSHIRE

Staffordshire has the unenviable distinction of being called the Black Country because of the smoke which used to pour from its factory chimneys. However, it has its beauty spots too. Staffordshire pottery is world-famous and other Staffordshire products are known internationally. Many of its former castles have now disappeared: Caverswall, Chartley, Eccleshall, Lichfield, Stafford, Tutbury (where Mary, Queen of Scots was imprisoned), and Newcastle-under-Lyme were among them. Lichfield has an impressive cathedral, even though it was battered in the Civil War and even more battered by nineteenth-century 'restorers'. Samuel Johnson, the great lexicographer and man of letters, was the son of a bookseller in Lichfield.

TAMWORTH

The site has a long history, for it was fortified by the redoubtable Ethelfleda, the 'Lady of Mercia', who resisted the Danes with great skill and success. William I gave the lordship of Tamworth to Robert Marmion who probably built the shell-keep. The Marmions were great warriors. Sir Walter Scott wrote an epic poem entitled *Marmion* which concludes with the stirring words:

> Charge Stanley, charge. On Stanley, on!
> Were the last words of Marmion.

In the fifteenth century Tamworth came to the Ferrers family. The castle was used by both Royalists and Parliamentarians in the Civil War but was not badly damaged.

Visitors will note the unusual herring-bone masonry, the Tudor banqueting-hall, the carvings and the excellent museum which holds many Saxon coins.

Tamworth Castle is off the A5, 15 miles from Birmingham. It is owned by the Borough of Tamworth and is open between March and September on weekdays 10 a.m.–8 p.m.; on Sundays 2–8 p.m. From November to February it is open on weekdays, except Fridays, 10 a.m.–4 p.m. and on Sundays 2–4 p.m.

Tamworth

SUFFOLK

Suffolk has a number of castles, mostly in ruins, but its chief glory is the number of 'wool' churches, which date back to the prosperous times of the Middle Ages when Suffolk people built large and impressive churches from the profits of the wool trade with the Continent. Like cathedrals, they were not made large and impressive to house large congregations, for the population of the area was insufficient for that, but 'for the greater glory of God'.

There is an impressive earthwork at Clare (in the town) and a 60 feet motte at Eye. The motte and ditch may be seen at Haughley, and a gatehouse at Mettingham and Wingfield. Ipswich and Walton castles have disappeared; the former through buildings, the latter overcome by the sea.

BUNGAY

Two towers and some walls remain of Hugh Bigod's great castle. It was once 90 feet high with 18 feet thick walls – much like the Tower of London. It now belongs to the Duke of Norfolk and is leased to the Bungay Town Trust which is diligently caring for it.

The castle is in the town and is open at all times.

BURGH

The walk is well worth it for you suddenly see the long walls – they were about 640 feet long and are still 15 feet high. The Normans built a small motte inside, but all surface traces have disappeared.

Burgh is a Roman fort, one of those built in the third century to fend off raids from Saxons and Angles. It is 3 miles from Yarmouth, along the A143, but there is about a ½ mile to walk when you have parked your car. It is in care of the Deparment of the Environment but is open at all times.

FRAMLINGHAM

Although what is left consists mainly of outer walls, these are extremely impressive, and it is possible to walk on them. The castle is late twelfth century and was built by Roger Bigod, Earl of Norfolk. The Bigods rebelled against the king on more than one occasion, but were allowed to keep

Framlingham is 19 miles north-east of Ipswich and 7 miles west of Saxmundham. It is a pleasant little town, with good facilities for tea and comfortable accommodation. The castle

the castle until 1306. Later it went to the Mowbrays and Howards, Dukes of Norfolk; both families were often in trouble, too. In 1636 the castle was given to Pembroke College, Cambridge, and much of the interior was used to make a poor-house. The thirteen bastion towers, which date back to 1190, are a spectacular feature of Framlingham.

is in the care of the Department of the Environment, and open:
15 March–15 October, 9.30 a.m.–6.30 p.m. daily including Sunday;
16 October–14 March, 9.30 a.m.–4 p.m.
Closed Maundy Thursday, Good Friday, 24, 25, 26 December and 1 January.

ORFORD

Orford Castle was built by Henry II in 1163 with the dual object of protecting the coast and keeping an eye on the Bigods (see Framlingham Castle) who were a constant source of trouble. Its 63 feet high keep was clearly the last world in military sophistication. It is circular on the inside but polygonal on the outside; the walls are 10 feet thick. It is unique. There were also other buildings and a large bailey with towers on it, but these have now gone.

A strange story belongs to Orford. In its early days a wild man of the sea was caught in the fishermen's nets. Efforts were made to make him talk by using medieval persuasion such as torture and hanging him upside-down. He looked human and ate normal food, but 'when taken into a church showed no reverence'! Once he escaped into the sea but came back of his own free will after a time. Later he escaped again and was not seen any more.

Orford, like other coastal castles, takes a little finding. It may be approached from Tunstall along the B1078 (6 miles) or from Woodbridge along the B1084. It is cared for by the Department of the Environment, and open:
15 March–15 October, 9.30 a.m.–6.30 p.m. daily including Sunday;
16 October–14 March, 9.30 a.m.–4 p.m.
Closed Maundy Thursday, Good Friday, 24, 25, 26 December and 1 January.
In the summer the visitor can usually obtain a cup of tea and a snack here.

Orford

SURREY

Surrey had two important castles guarding the gaps through the Downs at each end of the county. One was Reigate, of which no masonry remains and of which the site is now a public park in the town; the other was Guildford, of which more below. There is a small motte at Abinger, but it is on private land; the former castles at Betchworth, Bletchingley and Starborough have nothing of interest left above ground.

FARNHAM

Parts of the castle were made suitable for a bishop's residence but the Bishops of Guildford have not lived there since 1955, and parts of the buildings are now used as a college. There is much to see. Farnham has always been an ecclesiastical castle, but this has not prevented it being involved in military action on several occasions, notably in the Civil War. The keep at Farnham has foundations to the base of the mound. It is possible to see the well-shaft – and partly descend it. A rewarding castle to visit, and Farnham is a pleasant little town.

Farnham Castle is on the north side of the town, but finding it requires patience with the one-way system which, though no worse than most, seems designed to lure you away from the route you wish to follow. The castle is in the care of the Department of the Environment, and open:
15 March–15 October, 9.30 a.m.–6.30 p.m. daily including Sunday;
16 October–14 March, 9.30 a.m.–4 p.m.
Closed Maundy Thursday, Good Friday, 24, 25, 26 December and 1 January.

GUILDFORD

There is little to show the once-great importance of Guildford Castle, which controlled the Guildford Gap, a gorge cut by the River Wey between the Hog's Back and the remainder of the North Downs. The military significance of Guildford has been recognised throughout the centuries, and it was as vital in 1940 as it was in 1140. However, the castle has never had to stand a siege. It became a gaol, and apparently a very crowded and uncomfortable one, until Lewes was built in the early sixteenth century to take prisoners in Sussex.

Guildford Castle is in Quarry Street, in a public garden. It is open at all times but all that remains is the exterior of a keep, 63 feet high and 47 feet square. Near by there is a museum with interesting exhibits, including relics which belonged to Lewis Carroll (author of *Alice in Wonderland*).

SUSSEX

After William I landed in 1066, and before he fought against Harold, he established castles at Hastings and Pevensey having brought over prefabricated wooden towers for the purpose. After his victory over Harold, William sent out his barons to build motte and bailey castles at every important ford, hill, valley, and cross-roads which could have strategic or even tactical significance. Thus Lewes was positioned at a gap in the Downs and also at the highest navigational point of the Ouse. William had no intention of being swept back into the sea by a successful counter-attack. He moved ahead cautiously, establishing strong-points wherever he went.

Sussex, in the eleventh century, was a tangle of thicket, woodland and marsh. Vast areas were undrained and uncleared. But it was vital strategically. There were once castles at Chichester, Eastbourne, Ewhurst, Hartfield, Knepp and Rudgwick, but what remains is only of interest to an archaeologist. Herst-monceux, off the A271 between Lewes and Battle, dates from 1441 and is more of a manor house than a castle. It now houses the Royal Observatory, but the gardens are open to the public 2–5 p.m., April to October, on Mondays and Fridays.

ARUNDEL

The present Arundel is largely a nineteenth-century construction, but there is an eleventh-century motte and a thirteenth-century barbican. There are other minor survivals. However, Arundel is fascinating to visit. It is the residence of the Duke of Norfolk, who is the premier Duke and Earl of England.

The first castle was built soon after Hastings by Roger de Montgomery. It had a stormy time in the early days and was besieged twice. In 1580 it passed via the female line from the Fitzalans, Earls of Arundel, to Thomas Howard, Duke of Norfolk, with whom it has remained ever since. The castle was besieged for a third time in the Civil War and fell in 1644. It remained in ruins for nearly a century, then the work of restoration began, and continued until its completion in 1903.

It may seem strange that the Duke of Norfolk should live in Sussex, but this is explained by the Arundel connection. Most powerful families held land in a number of counties. The Norfolk family were sometimes in royal favour, sometimes out of it, sometimes rewarded, sometimes executed.

The castle is open at the following times:
1–25 April and 1–31 October: Monday to Friday, 2–5 p.m.; 28 April–25 May: Sunday to Friday, 2–5 p.m.;
26 May–31 August: Sunday to Friday, 12 noon–5 p.m.
No dogs.

BODIAM

Bodiam is like a dream of a medieval castle, well proportioned and set in a lily-filled moat. It was built in 1385 by Sir Edward Dalynrigge to guard against French raids and possible invasion up the River Rother. It was partly slighted after the Civil War, in which it played little part, but it became a ruin through neglect. Fortunately it was bought by Lord Curzon in 1917 and was restored at great expense. It was presented to the National Trust in 1925. There is an excellent replica of a siege gun in this magnificent and beautiful castle.

Take the A229 Hastings to Hawkhurst road and you will find the castle 3 miles south of the latter town. It is owned by the National Trust and open:
April to 31 October, 10 a.m.–7 p.m.; November–10 March, to sunset, Monday to Saturday.

Bodiam

BRAMBER

Bramber was one of the first Norman castles after 1066 and was in the possession of William de Braose (*see* Abergavenny). The mound is natural, although it looks artificial. The castle guarded the River Adur, which was navigable at the time and which supplied tidal water to fill the moat.

Bramber has two particularly interesting points. One is a *banquette*, a narrow shelf which an attacker

On the A283 1 mile east of Steyning. Open to the public from 10 a.m. to dusk in the summer months.

would reach only to find himself completely exposed and isolated; the other is a piece of overhanging masonry which dates from 1644, when the castle was blown up in the Civil War, on the 70 feet high tower. It is a fine tribute to mortar and building of Stuart times, and compares well with the leaning towers at Caerphilly and Bridgnorth.

HASTINGS

This is the place where William the Conqueror built his first castle in England, a wooden one made of prefabricated portions brought over from Normandy. The Battle of Hastings was fought subsequently at Battle, 6 miles away. The first holder of the castle was Humphrey de Tilleul, but his wife refused to join him and threatened to be unfaithful unless he returned to France. Henpecked Humphrey did so. The Count d'Eu then held it, but later it became a royal castle.

There are some curious dungeons at Hastings, at ground level. Guards could listen to prisoners' whispered conversation from the far end of the passage leading to the dungeons. The explanation of this acoustic phenomenon is not known, but is thought to be the accidental fluting of the walls of the rock passage. The guide gives a demonstration. The ruins are haunted.

The castle is on the cliff above the town. Over the centuries part of this cliff has disappeared into the sea, taking some of the castle with it. The existing remains are open to visitors from Easter to 15 October, 10 a.m.–5.30 p.m. The services of a guide are usually available.

LEWES

Lewes was built by William de Warenne who received huge grants of land for his services at the Battle of Hastings and elsewhere. He and his wife Gundrada founded the St Pancras Priory at Lewes and other priories elsewhere. Their coffins (empty) are in Southover Church, Lewes. Warenne was killed by an arrow at the siege of Pevensey Castle in 1088. The family became immensely powerful and became Earls of Warenne, Surrey, Sussex and Strathearn, but died out in the legitimate line in 1347.

The castle is unusual in that it has two mounds, though only one carries masonry. It is possible to

Lewes Castle is clearly visible in the town. It is owned by the Sussex Archaeological Society who have a museum close by the fourteenth-century barbican. The castle is open to the public all the year: on weekdays, 10 a.m.–1 p.m. and 2–5 p.m.; Sundays 2–5 p.m. From October to April it is closed on Sundays.

Lewes

ascend the keep and note how the castle controlled
the gap in the South Downs, the passage of the
navigable River Ouse, and a large area of
countryside. From the parapet the battlefield of
Lewes (1264) may be viewed very clearly (there is
an arrow pointing to it).

PEVENSEY

Pevensey was formerly the Roman town of
Anderida. At that time it was on the sea, and was
well fortified against attacks from Saxon raiders in
the third century. When the Romans left, the
Britons tried to defend Pevensey but were all
massacred. The Normans quickly appreciated the
value of Pevensey and built a castle inside the
Roman walls. This saw much action and there are
stone missiles on view, relics of some long-
forgotten battle. There is plenty of this castle to
see, and an interesting aspect of it is that in 1940 it
was strengthened against a possible German
invasion. Gun emplacements and pill-boxes were
built to blend with the external appearance of the
castle, which still looked a harmless ruin. An attack
would have proved otherwise. All these
modifications may be seen today although the
weapons have, of course, long since been removed.

Pevensey Castle is on the
A259 from Eastbourne to
Bexhill. It is in the care of
the Department of the
Environment and open:
15 March–15 October, 9.30
    a.m.–6.30 p.m. daily
    including Sunday;
16 October–14 March, 9.30
    a.m.–4 p.m.
Closed Maundy Thursday,
    Good Friday, 24, 25, 26
    December and 1 January.

TYNE AND WEAR

The metropolitan county of Tyne and Wear was created in 1974 from the industrial areas of south-eastern Northumberland and north-eastern Durham.

NEWCASTLE-UPON-TYNE

Robert, Duke of Normandy, son of William the Conqueror, began building here on the site, which had been fortified since Roman times, but the present buildings date from 1172; they include a huge keep with 16 feet thick walls. The original well, 100 feet deep, still yields water. In spite of its strength, Newcastle was sometimes captured, as in the Civil War by the Scots. Subsequently the castle had a long history as a gaol. There is a lot to see here, including a museum.

The castle is in the town. It is open to visitors on weekdays, except Mondays: between April and September, 10 a.m.–5 p.m.; from October to March, 10 a.m.–4 p.m.

Newcastle-upon-Tyne

WARWICKSHIRE

Warwickshire has the Shakespeare country (and industry), a number of impressive country houses – Coughton Court, Charlecote, Upton, Ragley and Compton Wyngates – the controversial new Coventry Cathedral, and two exceptional castles at Kenilworth and Warwick. There were once castles at Ansley, Baginton, Beaudesert (still a large earthwork), Brinklow (a motte and double bailey), Caledon, Castle Bromwich, Fillongley (2), Fulbroke, Coleshill, Hartshill and Wolston (Brandon Castle). There is a very attractive small castle at Maxstoke but it is not normally open to the public.

ASTLEY

The Astley family owned considerable land in Warwickshire when they built this castle in the late thirteenth century; their nominal rent for this manor to their feudal overlord, the Earl of Warwick, was to be on hand to hold his stirrup when he wished to mount his horse! In the fifteenth century it passed, by marriage, to the Grey family. Lady Jane Grey, the unfortunate girl who was made Queen of England by her scheming father-in-law, the Duke of Northumberland, lived here. After her short reign she was executed and the future Queen Elizabeth was lucky not to have shared her fate.

Astley Castle, after a period as a restaurant, was gutted by fire and now awaits restoration.

Astley is near Nuneaton, off the B4102.

Astley

KENILWORTH

Today Kenilworth Castle does not look very formidable militarily, for the 111-acre lake, made by damming two small streams, has been drained, but in its day it was virtually impregnable.

The first castle was built in the early twelfth century by Geoffrey de Clinton; he strengthened it by cutting a ditch across the spur of land, which can be seen. Fifty years later the massive Norman keep was built. In 1265 it was the scene of a siege which lasted a year, and which ended only because of famine and dysentery. In the sixteenth century the Earl of Leicester entertained Queen Elizabeth here for nineteen days, which cost him £1 million in present-day values. Sir Walter Scott's novel *Kenilworth* is an imaginative account of life in Elizabethan times.

Kenilworth Castle is on the north-west side of the town which is very close to other notable tourist centres such as Warwick and Stratford-upon-Avon. There is no shortage of accommodation or tea-shops in the vicinity. The castle is in the care of the Department of the Environment and open:
15 March–15 October, 9.30 a.m.–6.30 p.m. daily including Sunday;
16 October–14 March, 9.30 a.m.–4 p.m.
Closed Maundy Thursday, Good Friday, 24, 25, 26 December and 1 January.

Kenilworth

WARWICK

Although some of its owners met violent deaths, the castle has been lucky and has passed unscathed by enemies and despoilers. There is much romantic legend attached to its early days when it was a pre-Norman stronghold – thus the legends of the Bear and Ragged Staff, the Dun Cow, and Guy of Warwick's Porridge Pot. Soon after the Norman Conquest, Warwick came to the family of Henry of Newburgh. Two hundred years later it went to the Beauchamps, and the great towers were built by the Beauchamps, father and son (both named Thomas). The present names of these towers – Guy's and Caesar's – have no particular relevance. The Beauchamp chapel in nearby St Mary's Church, containing the family tombs, should not be missed.

From the Beauchamps Warwick went (by marriage) to Richard Neville, 'Warwick the Kingmaker'. He was killed at the Battle of Barnet, and the title and castle went to the king's brother, the Duke of Clarence (Shakespeare's 'false, fleeting, perjured Clarence'), who was drowned in a butt of malmsey at the Tower of London. Two more beheadings, and the title lapsed. It was revived and was later conferred on Francis Greville, Baron Brooke, whose family still hold it.

Various stages of castle-building, from the early motte to the later residential apartments, may be seen at Warwick. The Great Hall (62 feet by 45 feet) contains a full collection of armour; in other rooms valuable furniture and pictures are displayed. Outside, peacocks strut proudly on the lawns – as well they may.

The castle is close to the town centre of Warwick and, in fact, is close to the 'centre' of England itself, which is said to be Meriden, a few miles away. Kenilworth is 5 miles distant, and Stratford-upon-Avon 8 miles. Warwick Castle, which is owned by Lord Brooke, is open 1 March–31 October daily, 10 a.m.–5.30p.m., and November–February, 10 a.m.–4.30 p.m. Telephone inquiries to (Warwick) 0926 45421. Tea is available and a licensed restaurant. Warwick is so beautifully preserved and maintained that it gives an almost idealistic view of life in a medieval castle. Medieval banquets are sometimes held here.

Warwick

WEST MIDLANDS

West Midlands was created as a metropolitan county in 1974 by combining a sizeable piece of Warwickshire and Staffordshire. The aim of the changes which took place that year was to produce approximately equal administrative areas. Historical and sporting traditions were ignored and the new organisations are, it seems, neither as popular nor as efficient as their creators hoped. In some areas the changes are already under review and there is a strong possibility of reversion to the former names and districts.

DUDLEY

The first castle here was built soon after the Norman Conquest but this was demolished when its owner rebelled against Henry II in 1174. It was rebuilt, but some of its early owners were as foolish as they were unscrupulous and met unpleasant fates. It was besieged in 1644 and was slighted in 1646; however, more damage than the slighting was caused by a fire in 1750. Even so, there is plenty to see.

Dudley Castle is somewhat unusual in that until recently it housed a zoo on the premises. Although it is rare to find a zoo in a castle today, it was the custom of medieval kings to keep wild animals in cages in their castles. It is open daily from 10 a.m. to dusk or 7 p.m. according to the time of the year.

Dudley

WILTSHIRE

Wiltshire has Stonehenge and Avebury, various prehistoric graves and fortifications, modern military training areas, and Salisbury Cathedral. In the Cathedral library is one of the four existing copies of the Magna Carta, and also William Harvey's *Exercitatio Anatomica de Motu Cordis et Sanguina in Animalibus*, describing his discovery of the circulation of the blood. It is said that when he announced his discovery no one over the age of forty believed him! A remarkable feature of Wiltshire is Silbury Hill, west of Marlborough on the A40, which today is 130 feet high and 120 feet wide and which, in its oldest part, dates from 2145 B.C. At Devizes there are massive earthworks but the building on them is modern; Ludgershall, too, has large earthworks. Castle Eaton, Downton, Sherrington and South Cerney once had castles. Malmesbury Castle is now part of the Castle Hotel, and Marlborough Castle motte is within the grounds of Marlborough College.

OLD SARUM

The castle ruin is in the middle of an Iron Age fort, and the massive earthworks will leave the greatest impression on the visitor, who will observe that not only are there remains of a substantial Norman castle but also of a cathedral. Old Sarum was once a town, a bishopric, the site of an episcopal palace and a military centre. Because of conflicting interests, the military and the clergy could not see eye to eye in the thirteenth century, and a new cathedral and town of Sarum (or Salisbury) were built near by.

Old Sarum lies 1½ miles north of Salisbury and is in the care of the Department of the Environment. It is open:
15 March–15 October, 9.30 a.m.–6.20 p.m. daily including Sunday;
16 October–14 March, 9.30 a.m.–4 p.m.
Closed Maundy Thursday, Good Friday, 24, 25, 26 December and 1 January.

Old Sarum

As the new town grew up, Old Sarum still retained the right to be represented by two members in parliament. This became a great scandal in the early nineteenth century when towns like Birmingham had no representation at all. The abuse of 'pocket boroughs' (so called because they were in the pocket of a rich landowner) was ended by the 1832 Reform Act. Of all castles which one can visit, Old Sarum is one of the most rewarding. The visitor should take the opportunity to spend some time in the town of Salisbury itself. To see Salisbury Cathedral is an experience which should not be missed.

OLD WARDOUR

Old Wardour was built by John, 5th Lord Lovell (spelt variously), in 1393. It had a number of distinguished owners, such as the Duke of Clarence and Fulke Greville before it became the property of the Lord of Arundell in 1605. The Arundells were staunch Royalists and Catholics. Thus in 1643 Wardour, garrisoned by a mere twenty-five persons, was attacked by 1,300 Parliamentary troops. Its commander was Blanche, Lady Arundell, a woman of sixty, whose husband was at Oxford with Charles I. The gallant twenty-five held out for six days in spite of a heavy bombardment, mining, and blood-curdling threats. Parliament then garrisoned Wardour and put it under the command of Edmund Ludlow. But soon the castle was under siege again – this time from Royalists. Ludlow had seventy-five men and they held out for four months in a siege which even included hand-to-hand fighting. Wardour looks so peaceful and attractive today, with its grotto and lawns, that it is difficult to imagine these violent scenes in its history.

Old Wardour is 1½ miles west of Tisbury. It is in the care of the Department of the Environment and open: 15 March–15 October, 9.30 a.m.–6.30 p.m. daily including Sunday; 16 October–14 March, 9.30 a.m.–4 p.m. Closed Maundy Thursday, Good Friday, 24, 25, 26 December and 1 January. It is sometimes called 'Wardour' and, at other times, 'Old Wardour'. New Wardour Castle was built in the eighteenth century and does not concern us.

YORKSHIRE

Although the former county of Yorkshire has been divided into North Yorkshire, West Yorkshire, and South Yorkshire, and parts of the earlier county have gone to make Cleveland and Humberside, these administrative titles neither hinder nor help the visitor to castles; he will be guided by the road numbers and directions given below, for it is easier to appreciate the siting of Yorkshire castles if they are seen in relation to medieval Yorkshire and its military problems. There is a large number of ruined castles in the area, which include: Ayton, Aughton, Barwick, Buttercombe, Castleton, Cawood, Cotherstone, Cottingham, Crayke (built by a Bishop of Durham), Danby, Harewood, Kilton, Mulgrave, Northallerton, Pontefract (now only walls in a public park), Ravensworth, Sandal (recently excavated and of great interest), Sheriff Hulton, Tickhill (once famous and formidable), and Whorlton. Only the most dedicated castle-seeker will wish to search out all of these, and he will doubtless do it from his Ordnance Survey map.

There are particularly interesting abbey ruins in Yorkshire. One is Fountains, four miles south-west of Ripon; another Jervaulx, four miles north-west of Masham, and a third at Rievaulx, two miles north of Helmsley, though the ruins of the last are somewhat overshadowed by eighteenth-century additions.

BOLTON

Mary, Queen of Scots, spent part of her years in captivity at Bolton. In the Civil War Bolton withstood a desperate siege which ended because the garrison had eaten everything normally reckoned as eatable and some things which were not. Bolton is very impressive as one approaches, but only one half is in use; the other is a ruin.

Bolton is 4 miles from Middleham and 3 miles from Wensleydale. It is open every day, except Mondays, from 10 a.m. to dusk; but is also open on Bank Holiday Mondays. Since the fourteenth century it has been the property of Lord Scrope. There are a museum and a restaurant in the castle.

BOWES

Bowes castle stands in a Roman fort and still has a huge keep 50 feet high and 82 feet by 60 feet at the base.

The castle lies just south of the town. It is in the care of the Department of the Environment. Open 10 a.m. –5.30 p.m. Weekdays, Sundays, 2–5.30 p.m.

Bowes

CASTLE HOWARD

Castle Howard was designed by Vanbrugh in the early eighteenth century. Hawksmoor designed the mausoleum. The house is full of magnificent pictures, furniture and statuary, and there are costume galleries as well.

Castle Howard is 15 miles north-east of York, 3 miles off the A64 and 6 miles west of Malton. It is not a true castle in spite of its name. However, it is a magnificent eighteenth-century mansion, full of interesting exhibits, and is open to the public from Easter Sunday to the first Sunday in October 11.30 a.m.–5 p.m. daily.
There is a tea-house and a licensed restaurant.

CASTLE SPOFFORTH

William de Percy was rewarded by Spofforth for services in the Norman Conquest. The male line failed in the thirteenth century, but the name was continued through the husband of one of the female descendants. The principal Percy family then moved to Alnwick, and their adventures are chronicled under that heading. Some, however, continued to live here. Henry Hotspur, who was killed at the Battle of Shrewsbury in 1403, was born here. Much of the building has been removed, but plenty remains, including the great hall and under-croft.

Spofforth is 5 miles south of Harrogate. It is in the care of the Department of the Environment and open:
15 March–15 October, 9.30 a.m.–6.30 p.m. daily including Sunday;
16 October–14 March, 9.30 a.m.–4 p.m.
Closed Maundy Thursday, Good Friday, 24, 25, 26 December and 1 January.

CONISBROUGH

Conisbrough was one of the many possessions of the formidable Warenne family. William de Warrene was related to William the Conqueror, was 'remarkably valiant', and held vast tracts of land in various parts of England.

The most striking feature of Conisbrough is the huge keep, built by Hamelin de Warenne (Hamelin was half-brother of Henry II and became a Warenne by marriage to Isabel de Warenne, who 'held land in twelve counties'). The legitimate line of the Warennes, Earls of Surrey, Sussex and Strathearn, died out in 1347, but there were numerous illegitimate descendants, some of whom became Barons of Poynton in Cheshire. Unfortunately for the direct line, the last Earl, John de Warenne, abducted the wife of the Earl of Lancaster, and had other notable mistresses. The Warenne coat of arms, blue and gold squares, was borne by their illegitimate descendants (when authorised by the College of Arms). Apart from its own merits, Conisbrough is well known through Sir Walter Scott's novel *Ivanhoe*, though the reader will be well aware that most of the characters in that novel are fictitious.

Conisbrough is 4½ miles south of Doncaster, close to, but not on, the M1. As you approach the town the castle is clearly visible on the hillside. It is in the care of the Department of the Environment, and open:
15 March–15 October, 9.30 a.m.–6.30 p.m. daily including Sunday;
16 October–14 March, 9.30 a.m.–4 p.m.
Closed Maundy Thursday, Good Friday, 24, 25, 26 December and 1 January.

HELMSLEY

The castle, although ruined, is a splendidly impressive building and some parts of it have been restored to show what they looked like. The original building was begun in the twelfth century, and the fine keep dates from that period, although the height was increased later. The obvious strength of the castle, with its double ditches and double bank, seems to have deterred aggressors until the Civil War, when, in 1644, it experienced a three-month siege by the Parliamentarians, and surrendered after a long heavy bombardment. Its owner at the time was the 2nd Duke of Buckingham, who, when he returned from exile, married Mary Fairfax, daughter of Sir Thomas Fairfax, who had conducted the 1644 siege operations. After Buckingham's death it was sold to the Duncombes.

Helmsley is 15 miles from Thirsk on the A170 to Scarborough. The castle is in the care of the Department of the Environment and open:
15 March–15 October, 9.30 a.m.–6.30 p.m. daily including Sunday;
16 October–14 March, 9.30 a.m.–4 p.m.
Closed Maundy Thursday, Good Friday, 24, 25, 26 December and 1 January.
Helmsley is an attractive little town which welcomes tourists and is sometimes crowded.

KNARESBOROUGH

Knaresborough is rich in history, some of it macabre. An early owner (1170) was Hugh de Morville, one of the four murderers of Thomas Becket in Canterbury Cathedral. The other three fled here after the murder, but were pardoned after a year provided they made a pilgrimage to Jerusalem. King John was often here and in the war of 1215–16 crossbow bolts were made at the rate of 30,000 a year. The castle had many distinguished owners, including John of Gaunt. It was besieged in the Civil War and slighted after it. In the eighteenth century Knaresborough became notorious as the home of the scholar and murderer Eugene Aram who was hanged in chains here.

Knaresborough Castle is in the middle of a picturesque little town and, although a ruin, has much to show. The castle is open to the public from Easter to October, 10 a.m.–5.30 p.m. and there are guided tours of the museum.

MIDDLEHAM

A castle was built here soon after the Norman Conquest, but the present one was begun over a century later. It soon passed into the hands of the Nevilles, one of the greatest and most turbulent baronial families of the Middle Ages. The two branches of this influential family detested each other. The most famous member of the family was Richard, Earl of Warwick, known as the Kingmaker. He played a leading part in the Wars of the Roses (1455–71) until he was killed at the Battle of Barnet. After his death Middleham went to Richard, Duke of Gloucester, later Richard III.

There is a fine keep here and plenty of masonry, but the moat, which must have been vital to the defences, has been filled in, and an outer wall has been demolished; thus Middleham does not look very well protected today. There is an extensively illustrated booklet on sale here, entitled 'Richard III', which gives a good insight into fifteenth-century life.

Middleham lies 2 miles south of Leyburn, is in the care of the Department of the Environment and open: 15 March–15 October, 9.30 a.m.–6.30 p.m. daily including Sunday; 16 October–14 March, 9.30 a.m.–4 p.m. Closed Maundy Thursday, Good Friday, 24, 25, 26 December and 1 January.

PICKERING

Visitors to this region, where they may also see the castles of Helmsley and Scarborough, will probably

Pickering is 16 miles west of Scarborough and 7 miles

overleaf—Scarborough

be surprised to find so much natural beauty. Southerners are inclined to believe that the north is all slag-heaps and factories; a visit here soon dispels such ideas.

Although the site was fortified in pre-Conquest days, the present stone buildings date from the twelfth century; wooden fortifications were also maintained here for another 150 years. The castle saw action on various occasions, and was even invested by a Scottish invasion force in 1322. It was not used in the Civil War, and for much of its later life was either a prison or merely deserted.

A remarkable feature of this castle is the cross-wall which divides the castle into two halves, even running over the shell-keep. This enabled the defence to resist attack equally from either side.

north of Malton. It is in the care of the Department of the Environment and open: 15 March–15 October, 9.30 a.m.–6.30 p.m. daily including Sunday; 16 October–14 March, 9.30 a.m.–4 p.m. Closed Maundy Thursday, Good Friday, 24, 25, 26 December and 1 January.

RICHMOND

The visitor will immediately grasp the strategic importance of the site and will also be impressed by its beauty. The castle is a ruin, but there is a lot to see, including a magnificent keep and curtain wall dating from the eleventh century. The keep is over 100 feet high. There is also a fine example of medieval lavatories in what is somewhat

Travellers on the A1 will notice the turn to Richmond. The castle is off the B6274, 4 miles south-west of Scotch Corner. It is in the care of the Department of the Environment, and open:

Richmond

romantically known as the Gold Hole Tower.

Richmond's remoteness, rather than its strength, seems to have been its main protection, for it escaped both the Wars of the Roses and the Civil War.

Henry VIII made his illegitimate son, Henry Fitzroy, Duke of Richmond in 1525, but the lad died when seventeen. The title was conferred elsewhere but died out again. Charles II then revived it for his illegitimate son, Charles Lennox, and the title has stayed in that family ever since.

15 March–15 October, 9.30 a.m.–6.30 p.m. daily including Sunday; 16 October–14 March, 9.30 a.m.–4 p.m. Closed Maundy Thursday, Good Friday, 24, 25, 26 December and 1 January.

RIPLEY

The Ingilby family have lived here since the fourteenth century. Ripley was granted to Thomas Ingilby for saving the life of Edward III when hunting. Much of the castle was rebuilt in 1780, although the gatehouse is fifteenth century.

In Ripley, 3½ miles north of Harrogate, 7½ miles from Ripon. Open: Easter Sunday and Monday, 11 a.m.–6 p.m. then May–September, Sundays 2–6 p.m. and Bank Holidays 11 a.m.–6 p.m. Open daily July and August 2–6 p.m. Privately owned: Sir Thomas Ingilby, Bt.

SCARBOROUGH

The site was fortified from a very early period. The Romans had a signal station here; they used points like Scarborough to give warning of the sighting of Saxon raiders out at sea. However, in later years Scarborough itself was sometimes sacked. Inevitably, a place of such strategic importance would see more than its fair share of violence, and the 100 feet high keep, which had been built by Henry II, was often put to a military test. In the Civil War Scarborough Castle was besieged twice and severely damaged in the process. In December 1914 it was bombarded by the German navy. In addition to its military history, the castle was also used as a prison. George Fox (see Launceston Castle) was once imprisoned here. The Well of Our Lady, at the cliff top, was long believed to have special healing powers.

Scarborough is a vast, memorable castle in a superb position. It should not be missed.

Scarborough Castle is on a headland above the town, 300 feet above sea-level. It is in the care of the Department of the Environment, and open: 15 March–15 October, 9.30 a.m.–6.30 p.m. daily including Sunday; 16 October–14 March, 9.30 a.m.– 4 p.m. Closed Maundy Thursday, Good Friday, 24, 25, 26 December and 1 January.

SKIPTON

Skipton is owned by Skipton Castle Ltd, a local trust, and is a model of how such a national monument should be preserved and displayed. The visitor will obtain a forty-point itinerary and an imaginatively set-out history. Skipton was besieged in the Civil War for three years – and held out – and was subsequently repaired. There is no point in summarising here the excellent account of the castle which appears in the illustrated guide and which is given during the conducted tour. There is a hearth which could take a whole ox on a spit, and a seventeenth-century account book which lists the sum of £1-9s-4d for washing all the servants.

Skipton Castle is in the town and, in fact, towers above it. It is open every weekday 10 a.m.–6 p.m., except Good Friday and Christmas Day. It is open on Sundays 2–6 p.m.

Skipton

YORK

Both castles were originally raised in 1068. One, at least, was said to have been built in eight days. The Normans had a difficult time conquering the north, and wasted no time in trying to consolidate their precarious hold.

The early castles were of wood, and the present Clifford's Tower was built in the thirteenth century. It seems to have acquired the name from the fact that Roger de Clifford, a rebel against Edward II, was hanged in chains from it in 1322. In the Civil War the castle was held by Royalists until after their defeat at Marston Moor in 1644. It had already been much damaged by seekers of building materials in the previous century, and the interior was burnt out in a fire in 1684. However, there is still plenty to see.

York, as is well known, is more than a town; it is a representation of English history. York Minster is one of the finest cathedrals in Europe, and there are other medieval churches. The town walls are open for walks, except in icy weather, and there are four town gateways. On these it was the custom to impale the heads of those who had fought on losing sides. It is possible to feel you are seeing a medieval world yet still be very comfortable in modern York.

There are remains of two castles at York, but the one which offers most for the visitor is that which is known as Clifford's Tower – the remains of York Castle. It is in the care of the Department of the Environment and open:
15 March–15 October, 9.30 a.m.–6.30 p.m. daily including Sunday;
16 October–14 March, 9.30 a.m.–4 p.m.
Closed Maundy Thursday, Good Friday, 24, 25, 26 December and 1 January.
The other castle, on the west bank of the Ouse, is merely a mound, and the former bailey has been built over. It is known as the Old Bail.

York

123

SCOTLAND

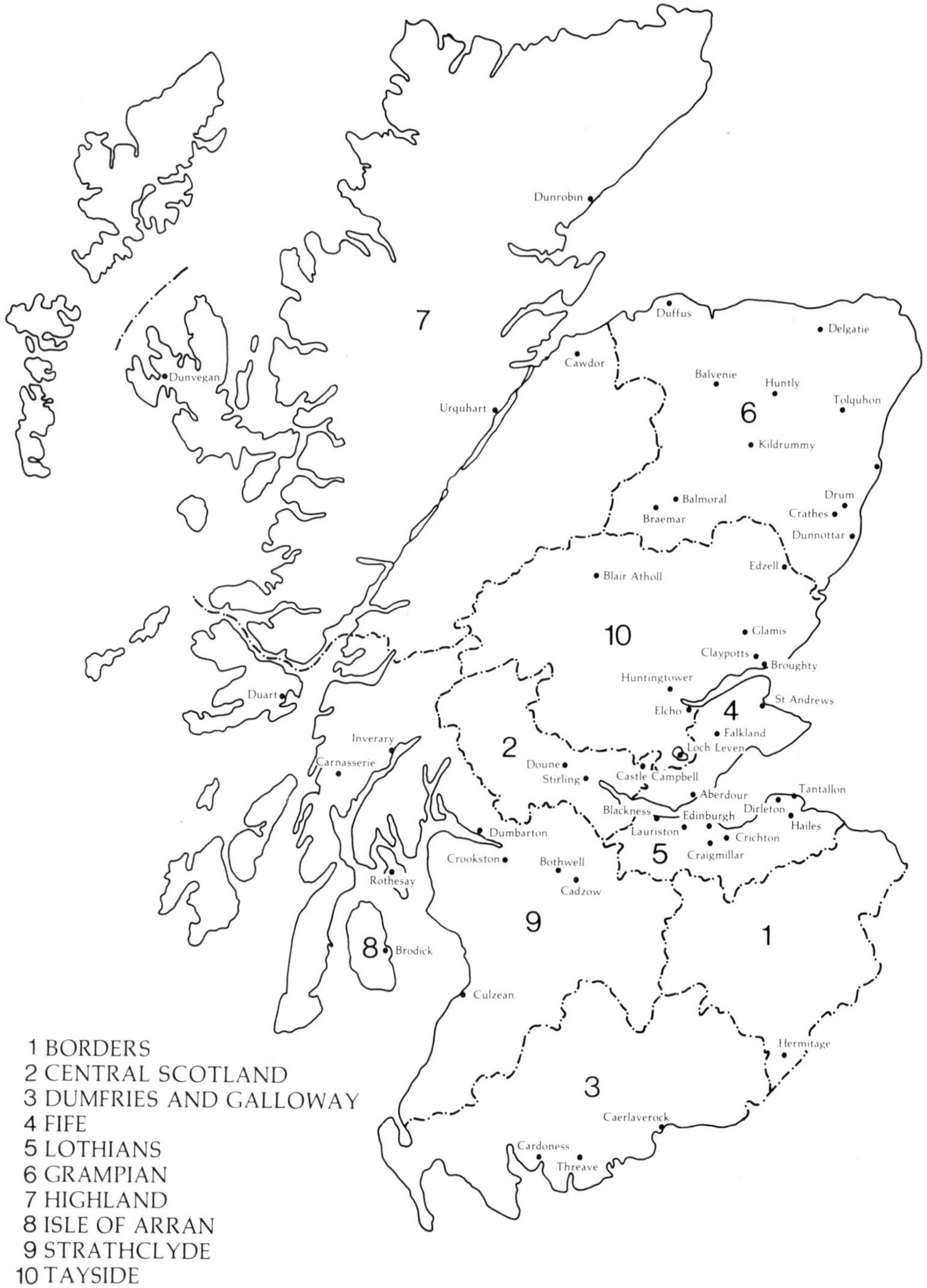

Dunrobin

Duffus
Delgatie
Cawdor
Balvenie
Huntly
Tolquhon
Urquhart
6
Dunvegan
Kildrummy

Drum
Balmoral
Crathes
Braemar
Dunnottar
Edzell

Blair Atholl

10
Glamis
Claypotts
Broughty
Huntingtower
St Andrews
Elcho
4
Duart
Falkland
Loch Leven
Inverary
2
Doune
Castle Campbell
Aberdour
Tantallon
Carnasserie
Stirling
Dirleton
Blackness
Edinburgh
Hailes
Lauriston
Crichton
Dumbarton
5
Craigmillar
Crookston
Bothwell
Rothesay
Cadzow
9
1
8 Brodick
Culzean
Hermitage
3
Caerlaverock
Cardoness
Threave

1 BORDERS
2 CENTRAL SCOTLAND
3 DUMFRIES AND GALLOWAY
4 FIFE
5 LOTHIANS
6 GRAMPIAN
7 HIGHLAND
8 ISLE OF ARRAN
9 STRATHCLYDE
10 TAYSIDE

7

There are a number of palatial castles in Scotland, such as Edinburgh, Stirling, Blair Atholl and Inverary, but even in more settled times they still give more than a hint of the Scottish motto *Nemo me impune lacessit*: No one provokes me with impunity. Most of the smaller castles give the message even more clearly; they are solid and sturdy, they dominate their sites, they are self-sufficient and they would be fiercely guarded by their owners, many of whom still live there. The setting is often wild and beautiful, on a crag, a cliff, or on an island in the middle of a loch. Often as you travel into a remote valley you will notice that you are under observation from an old fortification on a dominant point. Most Scottish castles and fortifications have a bloody tale or two in their history. Fighting was as natural to our ancestors as playing games is to youngsters today; there was not much else to think about and a raid was something to prepare and train for, something to look ahead to with a quickened pulse, and perhaps even a chance to gain a little plunder and prestige.

BORDERS

The region now known as Borders includes three-quarters of the boundary between England and Scotland. It has seen more fighting than most places. Both here and on the other side of the border in Northumberland you may encounter names like Red Valley or Blood Field that describe some long-forgotten battle or skirmish. Borders was formerly Berwickshire, although Berwick was not the county town; Berwick in its history has sometimes been a Scottish, sometimes an English, port. Duns gave its name to Duns Scotus, a medieval scholar and Franciscan who was born here in 1308 although he lived most of his life in England, France and Germany. When the religious dogmas of the church were questioned in the fourteenth century Duns was so resolutely opposed to new ideas that people who could not be taught or convinced became known as dunces – Victorian children were sometimes made to wear a pointed cap with D for Dunce printed on it. Duns has a fourteenth-century castle but it is not open to the public. Jedburgh was demolished in the fifteenth century after being the scene of many bitter battles; a prison was built on its site four hundred years later.

HERMITAGE

Hermitage was built by the de Soulis family in the thirteenth century, and as a vital border castle was frequently contended for by the English and Scots. The original builder, a man of diabolical wickedness, was boiled to death during a local uprising. Hermitage looks impregnable, but did not prove to be so. In 1338 it was held by Sir William Douglas, the Knight of Liddesdale, who starved his enemy, Sir Alexander Ramsay, to death in a dungeon here. Douglas's widow married an Englishman called Dacres, but the castle did not remain with the Dacres for long; however, they repaired it and built extensively. It was restored to the Douglas family, but they fell into disfavour again and Hermitage went to the Hepburns, Earls of Bothwell. In exchange the Douglases were given Bothwell Castle on the Clyde. Bothwell became Mary, Queen of Scots' husband, but was driven into exile. The castle holds an interesting bakehouse and an original garderobe (latrine).

Hermitage is 12 miles south of Hawick on the A7. It is open from April to September on weekdays 10 a.m.–7 p.m. and Sundays 2–7 p.m. From October to March it is open weekdays 9.30 a.m.–4 p.m.; Sundays 2–4 p.m. It is in the care of the Scottish Office.

CENTRAL SCOTLAND

Central Scotland was a vitally important strategic area and many were the battles fought for control of Falkirk or Stirling. The English suffered some heavy defeats here, at Stirling Bridge and Bannockburn, but won victories too as at Falkirk, where the mighty Wallace was betrayed by his own side.

BLACKNESS

Blackness was an important port. The castle dates from the fifteenth century and was a bone of contention between the Douglases and Crichtons. It was always a fighting castle, seeing action in the Civil War (captured by General Monk) and later developed for artillery fortification.

An interesting 'yett' (iron openwork door) and a particularly foul dungeon are part of the place.

On the south shore of the Firth of Forth 15 miles from Edinburgh on the A904. In the care of the Scottish Office and open:
15 March–15 October, 9.30 a.m.–6.30 p.m. daily including Sunday;
16 October–14 March, 9.30 a.m.–4 p.m.
Closed Maundy Thursday, Good Friday, 24, 25, 26 December and 1 January.

CASTLE CAMPBELL

The castle's situation, on a high rock with remarkable views, makes it unforgettable for the visitor. The great tower, its outstanding feature, was built in the fifteenth century. It was once known as 'Castle Gloom', in Dolour, by Grief in the Glen of Care. The name was formally changed in 1489 by the Earl of Argyll. The castle has seen

Castle Campbell lies 1 mile north of Dollar, off the A91, and is on the borders of the new area known as Central, and Tayside. It is now owned by the National Trust for Scotland but maintained by the Scottish

Castle Campbell

plenty of action, notably in the Civil War. It was burnt in 1654 by General Monk, the Parliamentarian, but subsequently used as a headquarters for English troops. In spite of demolition and neglect there is a lot of Castle Campbell for the visitor to see, quite apart from the external views.

Office and open:
15 March–15 October, 9.30 a.m.–6.30 p.m. daily including Sunday;
16 October–14 March, 9.30 a.m.–4 p.m.
Closed Maundy Thursday, Good Friday, 24, 25, 26 December and 1 January.

DOUNE

The castle was built in the late fourteenth century and, although never fully completed to the original plan, is one of the finest castles in Scotland. In the early days Doune had its fair share of executions and violence but escaped damage in the Civil War, though it was held for a time by Montrose. It was also lucky enough to avoid being damaged in the '15 and '45. Militarily the castle is of great interest, for the gatehouse tower, 95 feet high, contains most of the original features and was clearly entirely suitable for its purpose. Apart from the military side, the castle provides a valuable insight into medieval domestic life.

Doune is approximately halfway between Stirling and Callander, just off the A84. It is open April to October 10 a.m.–6 p.m. except for Thursdays in April, May and October. Visitors to the castle will also take note of the magnificent gardens, containing a Douglas fir 151 feet high, and the Doune Motor Museum which has a fine collection of cars.

Doune

STIRLING

The view from the battlements stretches over a wide area of countryside, and the river, whose passage the castle controlled, may be seen. It is a huge castle, in excellent repair, and is known as 'the key to Scotland'. Most of the buildings are fifteenth and sixteenth century.

Stirling is full of history and legend; it has changed hands on many occasions, usually through fighting. A castle was here in the eleventh century, perhaps earlier. It was very important in the thirteenth century and was captured by Edward I after a vigorous siege. Ten years later it was back in Scottish hands after the Battle of Bannockburn. In 1337 it was again with the English, and in 1342 back with the Scots. In 1452 James II of Scotland stabbed his dinner guest, the Earl of Douglas, believing the latter was plotting against the throne. The Stuarts were very fond of the castle and spent much time in residence. Stirling is so rich in history it is impossible to give more than a fraction of its story here. The castle also houses the Argyll and Sutherland Highlanders Regimental Museum.

Stirling Castle is in Stirling and open at the following times:

April, May and September: daily 9.30 a.m.–6.15 p.m.; Sundays 11 a.m.–6 p.m.

June, July, August: daily 9.30 a.m.–8 p.m., Sundays 11 a.m.–7 p.m.

October to March: daily 9.30 a.m.–4 p.m. Sundays 1–4 p.m.

Closed 25, 26, December; 1, 2 and 3 January.

Stirling

Dumfries and Galloway

Dumfries and Galloway region extends along that part of the boundary between England and Scotland which is not held by Borders, and along the Solway Firth out to the North Channel and Stranraer. This was the region of the Black Douglases. There were several branches of the Douglases and they all thought they were as good as one another and probably better than the reigning king; often they proved it.

Caerlaverock

As well as being beautiful in its setting, the castle is particularly interesting militarily owing to its unusual triangular design, based on the shape of a shield. It dates from the late thirteenth century. It was captured by Edward I in 1300, but recaptured by the Scots in 1312 from Edward II. In 1353 it was in the thick of more fighting, and again in the sixteenth century. It underwent its last siege in 1640, holding out for thirteen weeks against the Covenanters. Its drum towers, its early gun loops, and, especially, its brilliant strategic setting are notable.

Caerlaverock is 7 miles south-east of Dumfries on the B725. It is in the care of the Scottish Office and open:
15 March–15 October, 9.30 a.m.–6.30 p.m. daily including Sunday;
16 October–14 March, 9.30 a.m.–4 p.m.
Closed Maundy Thursday, Good Friday, 24, 25, 26 December and 1 January.

Caerlaverock

CARDONESS

This was the seat of the McCullochs of Galloway, but later went to the Gordons. It is a four-storey tower-house which has original stairways and fireplaces.

Cardoness Castle lies 1 mile west of Gatehouse of Fleet along the A75. It is open from April to September, on weekdays 10 a.m.–7 p.m, and on Sundays 2–7 p.m. From October to March it is open 10 a.m.–4 p.m. on weekdays and on Sundays 2 –4 p.m.

THREAVE

Threave was built in the late fourteenth century by Archibald the Grim, 3rd Earl of Douglas. It was owned by this branch of the Douglases, the 'Black Douglases', until 1455, when they lost it through defying King James II of Scotland. James brought up Mons Meg, the great cannon now on view at Edinburgh Castle, and battered Threave into surrender. It then became a royal castle, but the Maxwells were made hereditary keepers. In 1640 the interior was wrecked by Covenanters.

Threave is still 70 feet high and was once higher. Note the 'gallows knob' over the outer doorway – when the Douglases owned the castle it was seldom unoccupied. When a body swung from it it was said to be 'wearing its tassel'.

Threave Castle is a tower castle on an island in the Dee. It is 2 miles from Castle Douglas along the A75. There is no point in looking for a castle at Castle Douglas for there is none; its only connection with the Douglases is that they used to hang their opponents at Gallows Plot there. Threave is National Trust property and open to the public from April to September, daily except Thursdays. The Trust has established a school of practical gardening here.

Threave

FIFE

Fife has many attractions but to some it is principally renowned as the home of the famous St Andrews Golf Course. To others, it has many different interesting features such as St Andrews University, where students wear a distinguishing red gown, and it also has the only castle in Britain where a mine and countermine are still in existence. There are several stately homes in the district, such as Culross Palace, Kellie Castle, The Town House, and the Hill of Tarvit, all of which are well worth visiting.

ABERDOUR

The castle dates back to the fourteenth century, but there are many later additions. It was originally a tower-house, i.e. with sections built one above the other, and the site made it a strong fortress. Since 1342 it has been owned by one branch or other of the Douglases. The Douglases played a spectacular part in the turbulent history of Scotland as will be noted under other entries in this book. They held a number of different titles and it is interesting to note that one of these, the earldom of Morton, was granted in 1458 when James Douglas was betrothed to Mary, his king's daughter, who was deaf and dumb. In 1548 the Earl of Morton was Regent to Mary, Queen of Scots. He was implicated in the murder of Rizzio, one of her favourites, but managed to talk himself out of the consequences. However, he was subsequently executed for being involved in the murder of Lord Darnley, of which he may have been innocent. By the eighteenth century, Aberdour seems to have become very luxurious, with tapestries, curtains and rich silks.

The castle was abandoned as a residence in 1715, but was put to other uses, such as a school and a barracks: in 1924 it was taken over and restored by the government. There is plenty to see at Aberdour and this includes the gardens and a remarkable dovecote. In the nearby church you will find a 'leper squint' – the slot of the wall through which lepers, who were not allowed to enter the church, were able to witness a service. Leprosy, in those days, was thought to be highly contagious.

Aberdour, 7 miles north of the Forth Bridge on the A92, is easy to find. From April to September it is open on weekdays 10 a.m.–7 p.m. and on Sundays 2–7 p.m. October to March it is open 10 a.m.–4 p.m. and Sundays 2–4 p.m.

FALKLAND

There was a castle here in the twelfth century which belonged to the Macduffs, Earls of Fife. For a time it belonged to the Albany family, but they were all murdered or executed and it became Crown property. The present palace, which replaced the castle, is sixteenth century. In 1654 it was badly damaged by Cromwell's troops. In 1715 it was occupied by Rob Roy. The 3rd Marquis of Bute bought it in 1887 and restored the southern part. As it was originally the seat of the Scottish court, the phrase Falkland bred meant graceful and well mannered.

Falkland is 11 miles north of Kirkcaldy on the A912. The palace is owned by Her Majesty The Queen. The hereditary Constable Captain and Keeper is Major M. Crichton-Stuart, MC. The palace is open 1 April–31 October on weekdays, 10 a.m.–6 p.m. and on Sundays 2–6 p.m. Visitors are taken on a 40-minute guided tour.

ST ANDREWS

The castle was begun by Bishop Rogers in 1200, but it changed hands several times during the next hundred years. Sometimes it was held by the English, sometimes by rebels and sometimes by the lawful monarch. It has seen some grim events. Wishart, a Reformation preacher, was burnt here at the instigation of Cardinal Beaton, who watched the scene. Two months later, friends of the dead man captured the castle and displayed Cardinal Beaton's corpse on the battlements. John Knox was captured here, with the help of a French fleet, and sent to the galleys (1547). The outstanding military feature of the castle is the mine and counter-mine which were made in the 1546–7 siege, and are now floodlit and may be visited. The dungeon at St Andrews is said to be one of the worst in the world.

St Andrews Castle is a few hundred yards from the cathedral, with which it has always been connected. It is in the care of the Scottish Office, and open:
15 March–15 October, 9.30 a.m.–6.30 p.m. daily including Sunday;
16 October–14 March, 9.30 a.m.–4 p.m.
Closed Maundy Thursday, Good Friday, 24, 25, 26 December and 1 January.

LOTHIANS

Lothians contains the city of Edinburgh and the sites of some celebrated battles such as Pinkie, in 1547, which was an English victory and Prestonpans in 1745 when the Scots had their revenge. Of the castles in the region the most unforgettable is undoubtedly Tantallon. Edinburgh is justly renowned for literature, scholarship, architecture and medicine. Its fame as a centre of elegance and culture extends back through the centuries.

CRAIGMILLAR

There is much more left of this fourteenth-century castle than there is normally of castles of the same age. It was a royal castle and apparently very comfortable in its time; but, its reputation today has sinister undertones, and a number of people seem to have disappeared at Craigmillar. Its most famous association is with Mary, Queen of Scots. Near the castle is a group of cottages where her French attendants lived, and there is also the remains of an oak-tree she planted. The sinister aspect of her stay is that the plot to murder Darnley – her king-consort husband – was hatched at Craigmillar. Mary may or may not have been aware of the plot; she certainly had good cause to hate Darnley who had had her secretary murdered in her presence. She then married the Earl of Bothwell at Dunbar, but he came to a spectacular end too – in Denmark.

Craigmillar Castle is 3 miles south of Edinburgh. It is in the care of the Scottish Office and open:
15 March–15 October, 9.30 a.m.–6.30 p.m. daily including Sundays;
16 October–14 March, 9.30 a.m.–4 p.m.
Closed Maundy Thursday, Good Friday, 24, 25, 26 December and 1 January.

Craigmillar

Crichton

CRICHTON

The castle was begun in the fourteenth century, extended in the fifteenth and greatly altered in the sixteenth by the Earl of Bothwell. His additions are said to have been an imitation of those at the Palace at Ferrara. Architecturally it is very interesting and its history matches it. It was stormed by the Douglases after their young Earl had been murdered at Edinburgh Castle in 1440; it was again in trouble in 1483, 1559 and 1567. After the sixteenth century it fell into ruin and was in a poor state until it was rescued by the Scottish Office.

Crichton is on a hill 2½ miles out of Edinburgh on the A68. It is in the care of the Scottish Office and open:
15 March–15 October, 9.30 a.m.–6.30 p.m. daily including Sunday;
16 October–14 March, 9.30 a.m.–4 p.m.
Closed Maundy Thursday, Good Friday, 24, 25, 26 December and 1 January.

DIRLETON

Dirleton is a most attractive village and the castle ruins are especially picturesque. The first buildings date from about 1223, but were greatly added to in later centuries. Dirleton stood a considerable siege in 1298 when held by Wallace against Edward I, but its downfall came in 1650 when it was slighted by the Parliamentarian General Lambert. (Had it not been for the Civil War our heritage of castles would be much more complete, for most were damaged and some destroyed completely.) The ruins contain a seventeenth-century dovecote, with 1,100 nests, and a fine garden.

Dirleton lies on the A198 which runs from Edinburgh to North Berwick. It is in the care of the Scottish Office and open:
15 March–15 October, 9.30 a.m.–6.30 p.m. daily including Sunday;
16 October–14 March, 9.30 a.m.–4 p.m.
Closed Maundy Thursday, Good Friday, 24, 25, 26 December and 1 January.

Edinburgh

EDINBURGH

Doubtless a position like this must have been fortified in the Iron Age or earlier, but first records of the castle date from the eleventh century; Queen Margaret's Chapel, which you will see, dates from 1076. At various times in its history, Edinburgh Castle has been occupied by the English: Henry II, Edward I and Cromwell in turn held it. The castle was never taken by direct assault but by surprise, starvation, bombardment or the result of battles elsewhere. It has been the scene of dark deeds, treacherous murder and blind cruelty; over three hundred women have been burnt to death here for alleged witchcraft. The castle has museums and a great range of amenities. Not surprisingly, it is immensely popular.

Edinburgh Castle is on a rock 443 feet high, and seems to watch over the city. It is in the care of the Scottish Office and is open longer than many castles elsewhere. The precincts are open until 9 p.m. from June to September, except during the Military Tattoo. Otherwise, the castle is open on weekdays May–October, 9.30 a.m.–6 p.m. and Sundays 11 a.m.–6 p.m.; November–April weekdays 9.30 a.m.–5.15 p.m. and Sundays 12.30–4.30 p.m. In the summer the castle is thronged throughout the day with visitors of all nationalities.

HAILES

Hailes dates from the thirteenth century and is one

Hailes is 5 miles east of

of the most beautiful ruined castles in Scotland. It contains two remarkably unpleasant pit prisons into which visitors descend by ladders; it is not quite the same as being dropped into them, but it gives an impression of what it must have been like to be a prisoner in those times.

Although the Earl of Dunbar built the castle, the Hepburns, Earls of Bothwell, later owned it, and some of the family lived here. It has seen some brisk fighting – an attack by Harry Hotspur in 1400, which was beaten off, and a siege leading to its capture by Archibald Dunbar in 1443. In 1650 Cromwell slighted it, but there is still much left to see.

Haddington, off the A1, on the banks of the Tyne. It is in the care of the Scottish Office and open:
15 March–15 October, 9.30 a.m.–6.30 p.m. daily including Sunday;
16 October–14 March, 9.30 a.m.–4 p.m.
Closed Maundy Thursday, Good Friday, 24, 25, 26 December and 1 January.

LAURISTON

There was an earlier castle on this site, but the present one was built by Sir Archibald Napier. A later owner was John Law, who had a plan for a national bank of France accepted. The castle was much extended and civilised in the nineteenth century and is now a very fine house containing superb examples of the furnishings of that period.

Lauriston is 3 miles west of Edinburgh along the A93. The castle is open to the public between April and October every day, except Friday, 11 a.m.–1 p.m. and 2–5 p.m. From November to March it is open only on Saturdays and Sundays, 11 a.m.–1 p.m. and 2–4 p.m.

TANTALLON

The 5th Earl of Douglas was known as 'Archibald Bell-the-Cat' because of his habit of arrogantly telling people to do nearly impossible things. The Douglases, both 'red' and 'black', were a restless lot and were frequently in trouble – which suited them very well. In the Civil War Tantallon was captured by General Monk for Parliament. In spite of subsequent neglect, there is still much of Tantallon standing.

Tantallon looks what it is – a great castle with a violent history. It is on the edge of a cliff which makes it impregnable on that side, and there are deep ditches and tall earthworks on the other. At any time of the year it is unforgettable, but on a day when the sea-mist swirls round and the gulls dive and scream Tantallon – haunted, of course – seems to live again.

Tantallon Castle is 3 miles from North Berwick, along the A198. It is in the care of the Scottish Office and open:
15 March to 15 October, 9.30 a.m.–6.30 p.m. daily including Sunday;
16 October–14 March, 9.30 a.m.–4 p.m.
Closed Maundy Thursday, Good Friday, 24, 25, 26 December and 1 January.

overleaf—Balmoral

GRAMPIAN

In the Grampian region you will find plenty of interest at any time but if you can be there in early September you will see the Highland Games. Apart from robust athletics which include tossing the caber (a tree trunk) and exhibitions of sword-dancing, there is an accompaniment of pipes and drums which will not be forgotten by those who are present to hear and witness. This is the most entirely Scottish scene you will ever see and experience.

BALMORAL

Although Balmoral is really a Scottish baronial mansion, rather than a castle, it is on the site of a former castle and is clearly of great interest as the summer holiday home of the Royal Family.

In the early Middle Ages the site appears to have been occupied by a hunting-lodge. Later the Gordons built a tower here, and it then passed to the Farquharsons. There is a local legend that when they set off to battle each of the Farquharsons put a stone on a cairn; on their return each man removed a stone. The remaining stones showed the casualties.

Prince Albert bought the estate in 1852 for £31,000 and set William Smith of Aberdeen the task of building a suitable mansion in white granite. It contains a huge ballroom, but its most noticeable feature is an 80 feet high square tower. The surrounding scenery is magnificent.

Balmoral is on the A93, 8 miles from Ballater. The grounds are open to the public 10 a.m.–5 p.m. in May, June and July (unless members of the Royal Family are in residence) on every day except Sundays.

BALVENIE

Balvenie has had an eventful history. It has been destroyed by fire at least twice but nobody knows by whom and when. Its original builder was a Comyn, but in the fifteenth century it was a possession of the Earls of Douglas, the famous Black Douglases. There were many Douglases, including Red Douglases, and all were notorious fighters. Douglas castles may be found in various parts of Scotland. In 1440 William Douglas was treacherously murdered by King James II at Stirling; his brother James raised a rebellion to avenge him, but in 1455 the family was defeated

Balvenie, which is just to the north of Dufftown off the A491, is a thirteenth-century stone castle which has been added to since. It is now in the care of the Scottish Office and open:
15 March–15 October, 9.30 a.m.–6.30 p.m.
16 October–14 March, 9.30 a.m.–4 p.m.
Closed Maundy Thursday, Good Friday, 24, 24, 26 December and 1 January.

and lost all its estates. Balvenie was then given to the Earl of Atholl for an annual rent of one red rose (later increased to two!). After 1610 the castle passed through several hands and was frequently the scene of bitter fighting. In 1649 the Royalists were defeated at the Battle of Balvenie; in 1746 it was occupied by Cumberland's troops. It was also the scene of bloody battles arising from clan feuds. There is much to see at Balvenie, including the original iron gate, and interesting buildings.

BRAEMAR

Braemar Castle was built by the Earl of Mar in 1628, but in 1689 it was burnt by 'Black Colonel' Farquharson. It was rebuilt fifty years later and used as a garrison for English troops who added star-shaped battlements in the style of the day. Braemar has a round central tower, an iron gate and an unpleasant prison.

Kindrochit, also in Braemar and open at all times, dates from 1371, on a site with an earlier but little-known history. The Invercauld Arms stands on the site of the mound where the Earl of Mar raised the standard in 1715 and the exact spot of this event is marked by a plaque in the hotel. There are some eerie tales about Kindrochit. One is that plague broke out and the inhabitants were kept in while cannon destroyed it and them. There is a legend of treasure, but treasure-hunters are naturally wary.

Braemar, which is on the A93, has two interesting castles. Braemar Castle belongs to the Farquharsons of Invercauld and is open May–September, 10 a.m.–6 p.m. Son et lumière is staged from April to September. The castle is ½ mile north-east of the town.

CRATHES

Banchory is famous for lavender-growing and distilling; it is also close to the battlefield of Corrichie.

Crathes Castle is a late sixteenth-century L-plan tower-house which remained in the hands of the Burnett family until 1951. It is famous for its spectacular gardens, for its original interiors – once covered but now exposed again – for the horn of Leys dating back to 1323, and for its painted and oaken ceilings.

Crathes lies 3 miles east of Banchory, along the A93. It is in the care of the Scottish Office and open:
15 March–15 October, 9.30 a.m.–6.30 p.m. daily including Sunday;
16 October–14 March, 9.30 a.m.–4 p.m.
Closed Maundy Thursday, Good Friday, 24, 25, 26 December and 1 January.

DELGATIE

Turriff is known for the 'Trot of Turriff' – a battle in the Bishop's wars which preceded the Civil War. Here in 1639 a party of Royalists (Gordons) beat a contingent of Covenanters. Delgatie is a tower-house, begun in the thirteenth century, and added to in the sixteenth. It was the home of the Hay family for seven hundred years. The Chief of the Hay family became hereditary Lord High Constable of Scotland for services to Robert the Bruce; the Countess of Erroll, Chief of the Clan, holds the office today. The Hays were very martial and were renowned throughout the British Isles and overseas, but the family suffered a severe setback at Flodden in 1513 when those present on the battlefield, numbering several hundred in an age range from sixteen to sixty, were all killed.

Mary, Queen of Scots, stayed here and a picture of her hangs in the room she used. A notable feature of the castle is the painted ceilings (sixteenth century); but there are other exhibits, including a fine collection of armour.

Delgatie is 2 miles from Turriff, off the A497; it is open to the public on Wednesdays and Sundays 2.30–5 p.m.

Drum

DRUM

Drum was built in 1272 and given by Robert the Bruce to his armour-bearer, William de Irvine, in 1323. The castle has ever since remained in the family, and the present holder is the twenty-fourth of the subsequent line. The original castle was a crenellated tower but it was added to in 1619 by the building of a Renaissance mansion. The interior has decorated ceilings and the rooms contain portraits by famous painters.

Drum is 8 miles from Aberdeen along the A93. It is open to the public in June, July and August on Sundays only 2.30–6 p.m.

DUFFUS

Duffus was originally a motte and bailey but the present massive ruin is mainly fourteenth century. It was originally owned by the De Moravias, who became Murrays. Since 1705 it has been owned by the Dunbars.

Duffus is 5 miles north-west of Elgin off the B9012. It is in the care of the Scottish Office and open:
15 March–15 October, 9.30 a.m.–6.30 p.m. daily including Sunday;
16 October–14 March, 9.30 a.m.–4 p.m.
Closed Maundy Thursday, Good Friday, 24, 25, 26 December and 1 January.

DUNNOTTAR

The present castle was begun in 1392, but there was an earlier one on the site. It changed hands several times after fierce fighting in medieval times. It was attacked and damaged by Montrose in the Civil War; in subsequent centuries it saw considerable cruelty. In 1685 120 men and forty-five women were crammed into the Whig's vault – a dungeon – with the result that many died. This dungeon is now open to the public, as are certain other parts of the castle.

Two miles to the south of Stonehaven, on the A92, lie the vast ruins of Dunnottar Castle. It is open all the year 9 a.m.–6 p.m. on weekdays and on Sundays 2–6 p.m., except Fridays between November and April.

HUNTLY

The castle was originally called Strathbogie, at which time it was a wooden castle on the motte (by the side of the present castle), which was held by Duncan, Earl of Fife, in the twelfth century. A later Earl of Fife, however, quarrelled with Robert Bruce in 1300 and lost the castle, which then went to the Gordons. The Gordons became extremely powerful and were almost rivals to the monarch in their strength and prestige. The 4th Earl, who built most of the present castle, rebelled against Mary, Queen of Scots and the 5th Earl rebelled against James VI (in 1594) – both unsuccessfully. The result was that a portion of the castle was demolished; however, the Gordons were forgiven in 1597 and the 5th Earl was made Marquis of Huntly. He then began to rebuild the castle, adding many of its present

Huntly Castle is on the outskirts of the town of Huntly, 40 miles north-west of Aberdeen. It is approached via an avenue and is in the care of the Scottish Office and open:
15 March–15 October, 9.30 a.m.–6.30 p.m. daily including Sunday;
16 October–14 March, 9.30 a.m.–4 p.m.
Closed Maundy Thursday, Good Friday, 24, 25, 26 December and 1 January.

Huntly

very attractive features. His son, the 2nd Marquis, was executed for supporting Charles I.

Thereafter the castle fell into ruin, but since 1923 has been repaired and restored. Huntly castle is full of interest. Parts of it are outstandingly beautiful architecturally, and there are other parts which show the grimmer side of medieval life.

KILDRUMMY

The castle was built in the early thirteenth century and was apparently vast and strong. In 1306 Robert Bruce sent his wife and children here for safety in the care of his younger brother, Sir Nigel Bruce. It was besieged by an English force commanded by Edward of Caernarvon, later to be Edward II and later still to be murdered at Berkeley. He would also lose the Battle of Bannockburn in 1314, but at this stage, under the eye of his father, he was showing considerable military expertise. The castle fell because of the treachery of the blacksmith, who set it on fire. He had been promised 'as much gold as he could carry' and the English victors, who did

Kildrummy is on the A97, where there is a small car park for it. It is 35 miles west of Aberdeen and 3 miles south of Mossat, and is in the care of the Scottish Office. It is open:
15 March–15 October, 9.30 a.m.–6.30 p.m. daily including Sunday;
16 October–14 March, 9.30 a.m.–4 p.m.
Closed Maundy Thursday, Good Friday, 24, 25, 26 December and 1 January.

Kildrummy

not approve of treachery even if they profited by it, melted the gold and poured it down his throat. The garrison was hung, drawn and quartered, but Bruce's wife and children had escaped.

Kildrummy figured in other desperate sieges. In 1404 the Countess of Mar was seized at Kildrummy by Sir Alexander Stewart, illegitimate son of the famous Wolf of Badenoch. He forced her to marry him and declared himself Earl of Mar. This title was confirmed by King Robert III, and the new Earl certainly justified it both in battle and diplomacy.

Although Kildrummy is now a ruin and a shadow of its former self, it is still an imposing sight.

TOLQUHON

Tolquhon was begun in the fourteenth century. It is partly a fortress, and partly a gracious mansion. The exterior is formidable enough to deter any invader, but the interior is fit for royal visitors, whom once it entertained. The palatial part of the castle was built by William Forbes in the late sixteenth century.

Tolquhon is near Tarves, off the B4999. It is open from April to September on weekdays 10 a.m.–7 p.m. and Sundays 2–7 p.m. From October to March it is open 10 a.m.–4 p.m. and on Sundays 2–4 p.m.

HIGHLAND

Highland is a vast region which stretches from the Sound of Mull to Pentland Firth and from Cape Wrath to the Cairngorms. It includes scenery of astonishing wildness and beauty but much of it is difficult of access. The Highlanders were, and are, renowned for their hardiness, courage, hospitality, and ferocity when aroused.

CAWDOR

The Thanes of Cawdor (thanes were Clan chiefs) were well established in 1295 but their earlier history is not known. They are thought to have originated from Macbeth's younger brother. Their history includes murders, battle and kidnapping but more recently deeds of courage and national value. This and much more is in an amusing and informative guide-book written by the present Earl of Cawdor.

On the B9090 between Inverness and Nairn. Owned by the Earl of Cawdor. Open 1 May–31 September 10 a.m.–5.30 p.m. daily. Restaurant and snack bar.

DUNROBIN

The castle is owned by the Countess of Sutherland, but it is now used as a boys' boarding-school. Building began in the thirteenth century, but has continued in subsequent periods; the castle has also been restored after a fire in 1915. There is a very fine keep, and there are magnificent rooms in the modernised part. They house a museum and valuable paintings and tapestries. The gardens are modelled on those at Versailles.

Dunrobin is ½ mile north-east of Golspie along the A9. It is open to the public from mid-May to mid-September on weekdays 11.30 a.m.–6 p.m. It is closed on Sundays.

Dunrobin

DUNVEGAN

The castle is known to have been in the possession of the Macleods since 1200, but may well have been their stronghold three hundred years before that. This makes it the oldest inhabited castle in Scotland. The buildings have been added to in every century.

For most of its life the castle has only been accessible from the sea, but recently a ravine has been bridged to make a more convenient entrance. Although a vast forbidding fortress, virtually impregnable to attack, it has a palatial interior and contains many interesting relics, e.g. some of Sir Walter Scott's manuscripts. However, the most fascinating articles are the drinking-horn of Rory More, his two-handed sword, and the 'fairy flag'. The fairy flag is said to have been captured from the Saracens on a crusade. If waved, it will bring victory to the Macleods; this has happened twice. If spread on the marriage bed, it ensures children; and if unfurled, will bring herrings into the loch. It may only be used in emergencies.

Dunvegan Castle is on the western side of the Isle of Skye, off the A864. It is open to the public:
31 March–17 May, and 29 September–25 October daily 2–5 p.m.;
26 May–27 September daily 10.30 a.m.–5 p.m.
Closed on Sundays.

URQUHART

Loch Ness is a vast lake twenty-four miles long, and one mile wide. In parts it is 900 feet deep. It never freezes over. Urquhart was fortified in pre-Christian times. Remains of a vitrified fort were found here. Vitrified forts were made by burning together wood and stone; this became a solid impenetrable mass. Pieces of the old fort are in the museum here.

Urquhart figured in Edward I's Scottish wars, being captured and lost twice. It was constantly fought for later in the thirteenth century and the next two. Much of the latter period was occupied by a feud between the Macdonalds, Lords of the Isles, and the Scottish Crown. Urquhart was blown up in 1692 to prevent the Jacobites using it, and became very ruinous. However, there is still plenty to see in this huge, well-maintained castle.

Urquhart is 16 miles south-west of Inverness along the A82. It is on the shoe of Loch Ness and never lacks visitors. It is in the care of the Scottish Office and open:
15 March–15 October, 9.30 a.m.–6.30 p.m. daily including Sunday;
16 October–14 March, 9.30 a.m.–4 p.m.
Closed Maundy Thursday, Good Friday, 24, 25, 26 December and 1 January.

ISLE OF ARRAN

Arran has been described as an island of untamed natural beauty; (although a favourite holiday resort). It is twenty miles by nine, has a high peak (Goat Fell), good trout streams, and a mild climate. Robert Bruce rallied his forces here in 1307 and seven years later won a resounding victory at Bannockburn with them. Gaelic is still spoken. Arran is remote but accessible by steamer from Ardrossan, Glasgow and Fairlie. The bathing is described as invigorating.

BRODICK

As may be expected of the seat of the Dukes of Hamilton, Brodick is full of superb exhibits, notably paintings and silver. The present castle dates partly from the fourteenth century but mainly from the nineteenth.

Brodick is 1½ miles from Brodick pier along the A1. It is in the care of the National Trust for Scotland and is open to the public on weekdays 1–5 p.m. and Sundays 2–5 p.m. from 1 May to 30 September.

Brodick

STRATHCLYDE

Strathclyde is a huge area which includes such differing terrain as Glasgow and district and the mountains of Argyllshire. In the south it is good agricultural and cattle-raising country but in the north life is harder. Clan feuds probably originated for economic reasons – stealing food from a neighbouring valley to supplement your own – but eventually these feuds became institutionalised and had an almost religious fervour.

BOTHWELL

Bothwell was begun in the thirteenth century by the Murray family, and was added to subsequently to make it one of the largest and strongest castles in Scotland. The strategic importance of the site is obvious and the castle has seen plenty of vigorous action. It suffered a siege of fourteen months in 1298–9 and a shorter one in 1333. In 1362 it came into the hands of the Black Douglases. For a time it reverted to the Crown, then went to the Red Douglases.

It has long been a favourite subject with painters for it is a fine romantic-looking castle. There is a useful official guide-book on sale which contains much more information than we have room for here.

Bothwell is ¾ mile west of the town of Uddingston, 8 miles south-east of Glasgow. The entrance is along the banks of the Clyde, where there is a small car park. Most people will reach it by taking the turn to Bothwell from the motorway, but a few local directions would be helpful as the approach is slightly confusing. The castle now belongs to the Earls of Home, although it is in the care of the Scottish Office, and thus open:
15 March–15 October, 9.30 a.m.–6.30 p.m. daily including Sunday;
16 October–14 March, 9.30 a.m.–4 p.m.
Closed Maundy Thursday, Good Friday, 24, 25, 26 December and 1 January.

Bothwell

CADZOW

Begun during the eleventh century, Cadzow was a royal castle in the twelfth and thirteenth centuries, but temporarily became the possession of the Comyns; in 1314 it went to the Hamiltons for services at Bannockburn. It saw vigorous action in 1570 and again in 1579 when it was damaged and left unoccupied.

Cadzow is close to Hamilton, on the A71. It is open all the year round 9 a.m.–7 p.m. (or dusk if earlier), but visitors need to obtain a permit from the Estate Office at 18 Auchingramont Road, Hamilton.

CARNASSERIE

Carnasserie is a sixteenth-century tower-house, with traces of French influence on the architectural style. It is possible to visualise what the castle looked like in its more prosperous days. Its builder was John Carswell, who was the first Protestant Bishop of the Isles. His translation of Knox's liturgy into Gaelic was the first book in Gaelic to be published.

Carnasserie is 2 miles north of Kilmartin, off the A816. It is in the care of the Scottish Office and open:
15 March–15 October, 9.30 a.m.–6.30 p.m. daily including Sunday;
16 October–14 March, 9.30 a.m.–4 p.m.
Closed Maundy Thursday, Good Friday, 24, 25, 26 December and 1 January

CROOKSTON

There was a castle here in the twelfth century, but the present castle was built by Darnley, four hundred years later. Darnley (*see* Craigmillar Castle) and Mary, Queen of Scots spent their honeymoon here.

Crookston lies 3 miles south of Paisley and is owned by the National Trust for Scotland. It is open from April to September, on weekdays 10 a.m.–7 p.m. and on Sundays 2–7 p.m.; between October and March it is open on weekdays 10 a.m.–4 p.m. and on Sundays from 2–4 p.m.

Crookston

Culzean

CULZEAN

The whole area is a famous beauty-spot and the castle, built by Robert Adam in 1783 on the site of an earlier tower-house, is a fine example of the architecture of the period. The Kennedy family lived here, but they were a turbulent clan and two branches clashed violently. The head of the clan is the Marquis of Ailsa who lives near by. The castle contains the National Guest Flat which was given to General Eisenhower, Supreme Commander Allied Forces in World War II, for his lifetime.

Culzean Castle is south of Culzean Bay on the Ayr to Turnberry road. If you have to ask directions locally you should pronounce the name 'Cullane'. It is cared for by the National Trust for Scotland and is open from April to September 10 a.m.– 6 p.m. every day; and in October 10 a.m.– 4.p.m. Tea available.

DUART

The main part of the castle, the keep, is thirteenth century, but there were later additions. The Chief of the Clan Maclean lives at the castle, and has done much to restore it. The Macleans can trace their ancestry back to misty antiquity, but the builder of the keep was thirteenth-century Gillean of the Battleaxe. He was followed by a series of other colourful – some would say ruffianly – characters: Ian the Toothless, Red Hector of the Battles, Alan of the Straws, and the Pirate. Many desperate battles were fought with rival clans, notably the Campbells. One of the most

Duart is on the Isle of Mull and is most easily approached from the sea; there are numerous ferry trips which call here. It is open to the public from May to September on weekdays 11.30 a.m.–6 p.m. During July and August it is also open on Sundays 2.30–6 p.m.

remarkable Macleans was Sir Lachlan who, in the sixteenth century, disapproved of his mother's remarriage. He therefore murdered eighteen of the guests and imprisoned the bridegroom, thus safeguarding his own chieftainship of the clan.

After Culloden the Macleans were driven into exile and the castle was devastated as part of the Highland 'clearances', but in 1911 the Macleans repurchased Duart. Most of the restoration was done by Sir Fitzroy Maclean who lived from 1835 to 1937 – not many of the Maclean family could expect to live to the age of 102!

DUMBARTON

In 1305 Sir John de Menteith, the governor, treacherously captured Sir William Wallace, who was then executed: this occasion is brought to mind by the terms Wallace Guardhouse and Wallace's Seat (the higher of the two peaks). In 1571 the castle was the scene of an astonishing feat by Thomas Crawford who with a hundred men scaled the least accessible side and captured it from the supporters of Mary, Queen of Scots. One of the climbers was seized with a paralytic fit and his fellows had to ascend over his body, which they had lashed to the ladder, being unable to take it up or down.

Most of Dumbarton Castle dates from the fifteenth century and later.

Overlooking Dumbarton is a 240 feet rock, which has had fortifications on it from early times. The present castle is in the care of the Scottish Office and open:
15 March–15 October, 9.30 a.m.–6.30 p.m. daily including Sunday;
16 October–14 March, 9.30 a.m.–4 p.m.
Closed Maundy Thursday, Good Friday, 24, 25, 26 December and 1 January.

Dumbarton

Inverary

INVERARY

Home of the Duke of Argyll and the headquarters of the Clan Campbell, but the present castle was built in the late eighteenth century. It contains armour, tapestry, pictures and furniture. Although not medieval it gives a good idea of the appearance of some medieval castles.

On the A83 at Inverary. In November 1975 the castle was swept by a damaging fire but is now restored and open:
5 April–28 June (except Friday) 10 a.m.–12.30, 2–6 p.m.
29 June–26 September daily 10 a.m.–6 p.m., Sundays 2–6 p.m.
Tea available.

ROTHESAY

Rothesay is interesting partly for its circular shape and partly for its violent history. It is an early shell-keep which was probably built in the eleventh century and strengthened in following years. Shell-keeps are familiar in England, but this one is unique in Scotland.

Its early fighting was against the Norsemen, and it was captured by King Haakon of Norway in 1263; however it was soon in Scottish hands again. It saw more fighting in the next century and changed hands twice in the Civil War. It was burnt in 1685 but fortunately the 2nd and 3rd Marquises of Bute spent much thought and money on restoring it. There is much to see, and it is all evocative of Scottish history. On a slightly different note, the 'bloody stair' is where a reluctant bride decided she could not face her bridegroom and stabbed herself.

Rothesay Castle is on the Isle of Bute. It is now in the care of the Scottish Office and open:
15 March–15 October, 9.30 a.m.–6.30 p.m. daily including Sunday;
16 October–14 March, 9.30 a.m.–4 p.m.
Closed Maundy Thursday, Good Friday, 24, 25, 26 December and 1 January.

TAYSIDE

Tayside includes some notable distilleries and the impressive Scone Palace at Perth (rebuilt in 1803 on a historic site). Scone, pronounced 'Scoon', was the place where Scottish kings were crowned and the famous stone is now in Westminster Abbey. Scone Palace is open daily from April to October 10 a.m.–6 p.m., Sundays 2–6 p.m. Gleneagles, with its famous golf course, is in Tayside, and this too is a renowned district for salmon and trout fishing, grouse shooting and deer stalking.

BLAIR ATHOLL

Although the first castle was built in 1269, the present buildings date from 1768. Its present appearance gives little hint of the resistance it put up to the Parliamentarians in the Civil War, nor of the sieges it saw in 1745. It was, in fact, the last castle in the British Isles to be besieged.

It is the residence of the Duke of Atholl, but thirty-two rooms are open to the public. They are full of fine furniture and pictures, arms, china, tapestries and other interesting relics. The visitor is well catered for, and the castle is extremely popular as a place to see.

On the A9, 8 miles north of Pitlochry. Open from 1st Sunday in May to 2nd Sunday in October; weekdays 10 a.m.–6 p.m., Sundays 2-6 p.m. Open in April on Sundays and Mondays, also Easter weekend.

Blair Atholl

BROUGHTY

Broughty, which dates from the fifteenth century, soon began its long career of military adventure. In 1547 the English captured it after the Battle of Pinkie, but in 1550 it was retaken by a combined Scottish and French army. Towards the end of the Civil War it was captured by General Monk of the Parliamentarian forces. It then fell into ruin, but in 1855 the War Office bought it and rebuilt it as a coastal fort. Part of it is now a museum dealing with the history of the whaling industry.

Broughty is 2 miles from Dundee along the A92. It is open all the year on Mondays, Thursdays and Saturdays 11 a.m.–1 p.m. and 2–5 p.m. From 15 June to 15 September it is open on Sundays 2–5 p.m.

CLAYPOTTS

Claypotts is of special interest because it is one of the most complete Z-plan tower-houses. It was built in the sixteenth century and the architect intended to combine defensive capability with living comfort. Its relatively uneventful history has helped to keep it in good repair. Although in Scottish Office care, Claypotts belongs to the Earls of Home.

Claypotts is 1 mile from Broughty Ferry along the Arbroath road. It is in the care of the Scottish Office and open:
15 March–15 October, 9.30 a.m.–6.30 p.m. daily including Sunday;
16 October–14 March, 9.30 a.m.–4 p.m.
Closed Maundy Thursday, Good Friday, 24, 25, 26 December and 1 January.

EDZELL

Macbeth is thought to have come this way after Dunsinane (where, contrary to Shakespeare, he was not killed) and made his way to Lumphanan where he met defeat and death. Macbeth, incidentally, was a good king and very different from the character in the play. The building was begun in the eleventh century by the Stirlings of Glenesk. The Stirlings transferred it to the Lindsays in the early fourteenth century. In the sixteenth century the Lindsays moved out of the old castle into the nearby new one which was made quite magnificent, at vast expense, by Sir David Lindsay in the early 1600s. He left staggering debts and eventually in 1715 the castle was owned by the York Building Company who began to demolish it. Soon the York Building Company were also bankrupt and more of the castle went to pay their

Edzell is 6 miles north of Brechin on the B996; the castle is a mile west of the village. It is now in the care of the Scottish Office and open:
15 March–15 October, 9.30 a.m.–6.30 p.m. daily including Sunday;
16 October–14 March, 9.30 a.m.–4 p.m.
Closed Maundy Thursday, Good Friday, 24, 25, 26 December and 1 January.

debts. However, from the end of the nineteenth century devastation was stopped, and in the care of the Department of the Environment and the Scottish Office much repair and restoration have been accomplished. A notable feature is the Pleasance, a unique walled garden with symbolic sculptures created by the extravagant Sir David; he may have left huge debts, but posterity certainly owes him one, too.

ELCHO

There was a castle on this site in medieval times for William Wallace is said to have used it, but the present castle is a sixteenth-century fortified mansion. It has belonged to the Wemyss family since at least 1468, and still does. Elcho has seen rough military action but is very well preserved. As a mansion it had windows rather than loopholes; these were effectively protected by the iron grilles which may be seen today.

Elcho Castle is 3 miles south-east of Perth, on the south bank of the Tay. It is open to the public from April to September on weekdays 10 a.m.–7 p.m., from October to May 10 a.m.–4 p.m. and Sundays 2–4 p.m.

GLAMIS

Parts of the castle, such as the square tower, which has 15 feet thick walls, are very old, but most of it is seventeenth century. There is a museum and much else to see in the castle; outside there are superb gardens. Glamis has a reputation for dark and sinister deeds. King Malcolm II is said to have been murdered here in 1034. In 1537 Lady Glamis was burnt for witchcraft and apparently plotting to kill James V; subsequently she was proved innocent. There is a legend of a secret chamber where a monster child was kept and finally walled up. However there is a happier side to Glamis. The Royal Family spent much of their childhood here, and Princess Margaret was born at the castle.

Glamis is 12 miles north of Dundee, at the junction of the A94 and A298. Glamis is the home of the Queen Mother, but is open to the public at Easter weekend and from May to September on Sundays, Mondays, Tuesdays, Wednesdays, Thursdays and Bank Holidays 1–5 p.m. From 1 July it is open on Fridays also.

HUNTINGTOWER

It consists of two fifteenth-century towers 9 feet 6 inches apart. The space in between is known as

Huntingtower is 3 miles north-west of Perth on the

'maiden's leap' as the daughter of one of the Ruthvens, who lived there, jumped the space between the two towers rather than be caught in her lover's room. For a standing jump in the dark it was no mean feat. Later she eloped with her lover and married him.

The Ruthvens were often in trouble. One took part in the murder of Rizzio, the Secretary of Mary, Queen of Scots, in 1566. In 1582, the sixteen-year-old James VI (later James I of England) was 'persuaded' to dismiss his favourites. The Ruthvens by this time held the Earldom of Gowrie, but three years later the Earl was executed by James VI, who now felt more powerful: three years earlier he had burst into tears. The last Earl of Gowrie and his brother, suspected of witchcraft and conspiracy, were hung, drawn and quartered in 1600. Pieces of their bodies were displayed in various towns. The surname Ruthven was abolished, and the castle – until that time known as Ruthven Castle – was renamed Huntingtower. Subsequently it had a variety of owners. There are excellent painted ceilings here.

A85. It is in the care of the Scottish Office and open:
15 March–15 October, 9.30 a.m.–6.30 p.m. daily including Sunday;
16 October–14 March, 9.30 a.m.–4 p.m.
Closed Maundy Thursday, Good Friday, 24, 25, 26 December and 1 January.

LOCH LEVEN

The tower and certain other parts of the castle date from the fourteenth century. In 1335 an English army tried to submerge it by damming the River Leven and raising the loch level; they did not succeed. Mary, Queen of Scots, was imprisoned here in 1567. She was not well treated, but managed to persuade her gaoler to help her escape. However, her freedom was short-lived.

Loch Leven Castle is on an island in the loch, which is close to the M90 at Kinross. The island was once much smaller, but the lowering of the loch water has now made it approximately 3 miles by 2 miles. The castle is reached by ferry. It is open during the summer 10 a.m.–6 p.m. on weekdays, and 2–6 p.m. on Sundays.

Loch Leven

157

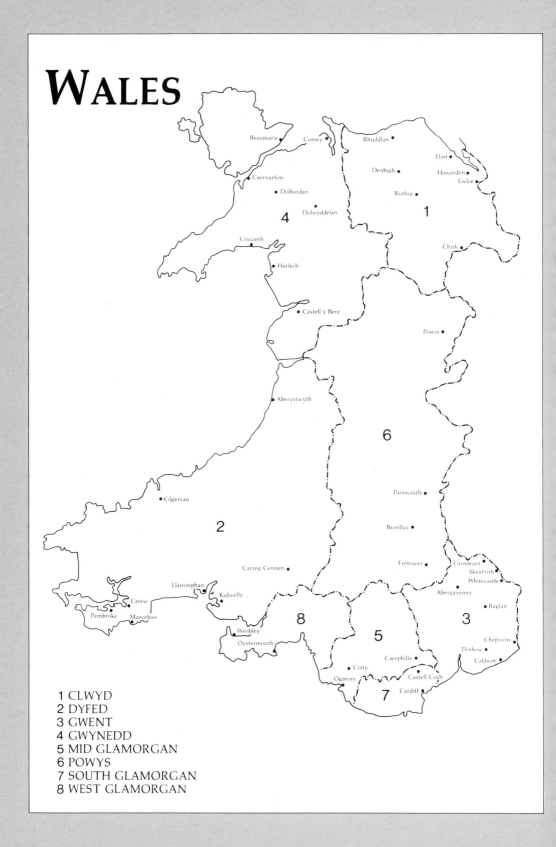

WALES

1 CLWYD
2 DYFED
3 GWENT
4 GWYNEDD
5 MID GLAMORGAN
6 POWYS
7 SOUTH GLAMORGAN
8 WEST GLAMORGAN

There are two main types of castles in Wales. There are the small fighting castles, many of which once covered an area larger than the one today but which are still small in comparison to the others. Then there are the great Edwardian castles, which were originally built to hold garrisons but were so ingeniously designed that they could be held by a surprisingly small number of soldiers. These are Conwy, Caernarfon, Beaumaris, Rhuddlan and Harlech. There were once others of equal majesty but time has helped obliterate most of them.

Castles along the Welsh border date from the days when the Marches (march = frontier) were the scenes of almost continuous warfare. The border between England and Wales was not clearly delineated (in spite of Offa's Dyke) and castles and sympathies often changed allegiance. Sometimes English border families took Welsh wives and became more Welsh than the Welsh themselves.

CLWYD

Clwyd, pronounced 'cloo-id', means a gate but invaders of this part of Wales from the Romans onwards did not find it was one which opened very easily, if at all. Clwyd stretches from Chester to Colwyn Bay and south to the Berwyn Hills. When Henry II invaded Wales in 1169 his army met a storm of such ferocity in the Berwyn Hills that it knocked all the heart out of the soldiers. Like all mountainous regions, Wales gets a fair share of rain but the good days make up for the bad ones. In Wales it is worth knowing that 'caer' means a hill and 'aber' a river mouth. 'Afon' is a river, 'bryn' is a hill, 'dinas' a fort, 'castell' a castle and 'carreg' a stone. 'Nant' is a stream and a 'cwm' (pronounced coom) a valley.

This land has seen many battles, large and small.

CHIRK

Lt-Col Ririd Myddleton's family has lived here since 1595. The castle was captured in the Civil War and the then Major-General Myddleton had to besiege it to recapture it, which he tried to do without damaging it; he was not successful but eventually it was surrendered.

Previously Chirk had passed through many hands, among them Mortimers, Arundels, Beauchamps, Henry VIII and Elizabeth I.

Today it is beautifully kept. Note those massive Edwardian drum-towers, probably of 1310. At that time the porter received twopence a day wages but you could buy a whole sheep for a shilling (the modern 5p) which was six days' wages at twelve pence to the shilling!

Chirk Castle is 4 miles from Llangollen off the B4500, and 2 miles from Chirk itself on the A5. There is a most impressive entrance drive. It is managed by the Welsh Office for the National Trust. Open:
5 April–26 October, Wednesdays, Thursdays, Saturdays and Sundays 2–5 p.m. and from June to September, Wednesdays, Thursdays 11 a.m.–5 p.m. Open all Bank Holiday weekends.

DENBIGH

Although a ruin, there is much to see and militarily it is particularly interesting. There was an early castle here, held by Dafydd ap Gruffyd, brother of Llewellyn III, but the present castle was mainly built by Henry de Lacy after 1283. Many of its early owners died violent deaths unconnected with the sieges which frequently took place around it. Its finest hour – or rather year – was in 1645–6 when it was besieged by Parliamentary forces. The castle was slighted, but it is still possible to see the postern and sallyport, the barbican at the rear (the

Denbigh Castle is in the middle of the town. It is in the care of the Welsh Office and open:
15 March–15 October, 9.30 a.m.–6.30 p.m. daily including Sunday;
16 October–14 March, 9.30 a.m.–4 p.m.
Closed Maundy Thursday, Good Friday, 24, 25, 26 December and 1 January.

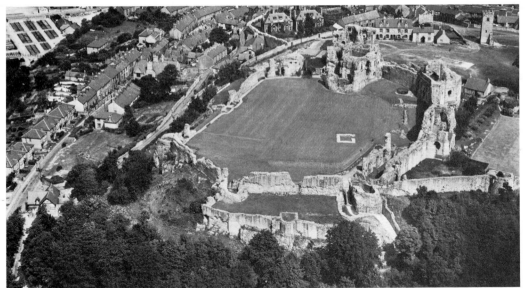

Denbigh

front one was demolished), and the gatehouse. The gatehouse with its triple towers, its portcullises and *meurtrières*, was the outstanding feature of this very strong castle. There were also underground passages and store-rooms. Denbigh, superbly situated, was in every way the military man's concept of what a fighting castle should be.

H. M. Stanley, who found Dr Livingstone in Africa, was born in Denbigh though he went to America and became an American later. There is a memorial to him in the castle museum.

EWLOE

The castle's situation in a valley may seem tactically extraordinary – as it is so different from other, more conspicuous castles – but it seems that the site was chosen so that the castle might not be immediately obvious to invaders.

The date of the first fortification on this site is not known, but it may be as early as the ninth century, and it is thought to have been made by the English. However, in the twelfth century it was used by the Welsh, and the Welsh certainly strengthened it in the thirteenth century. By the fourteenth century it had ceased to be useful and was allowed to decay, but the modern visitor will find much to see and much to puzzle him.

Ewloe Castle is 10 miles south-east of Holywell just off the A55. It is approached by a path across a field. It is now in the care of the Welsh Office and open:
15 March–15 October, 9.30 a.m.–6.30 p.m. daily including Sunday;
16 October–14 March, 9.30 a.m.–4 p.m.
Closed Maundy Thursday, Good Friday, 24, 25, 26 December and 1 January.

overleaf—Ruthin

FLINT

Flint was the first of the great Edwardian castles of Wales and was built at great speed by massing all available resources. Although now a ruin there is plenty of masonry and it is possible to see the original pattern, which included a large circular keep with walls 23 feet thick at the base. It was attacked by Llewellyn in 1282 – two years after completion – and it had a busy time in the Civil War. It was slighted in 1652. Richard II, who was later murdered by his cousin, the future Henry IV, was persuaded to abdicate at Flint. There is an extraordinary story concerning Richard's bloodhound which until that time hardly left his side. While Richard was talking to Henry the bloodhound ran to the latter and fawned on him. The event seemed symbolic to Richard, and he said so at the time.

Flint Castle is north of the town, on the Dee estuary. It is in the care of the Welsh Office and open:
15 March–15 October, 9.30 a.m.–6.30 p.m. daily including Sunday;
16 October–14 March, 9.30 a.m.–4 p.m.
Closed Maundy Thursday, Good Friday, 24, 25, 26 December and 1 January.

HAWARDEN

The castle which you see today is late thirteenth century, but there were earlier fortifications on this site, at least as early as the Roman period. It has seen considerable fighting. The castle you will visit is what is known as 'the old castle', which is on top of the hill; below is a magnificent eighteenth-century house, formally called Broadlane Hall, but now referred to as 'the castle'. It is owned and lived in by the Gladstones (the family of the nineteenth-century Prime Minister).

The old castle twice changed hands in the Civil War. Looking at the immensely strong position, surrounded by two ditches and a double bank and with walls in the keep which are 15 feet thick, it seems to be impregnable. Possibly its weakness was its water-supply for no traces of a well have ever been found.

Hawarden is 10 miles south-east of Holywell on the A55 (Chester–Conwy). It is open to the public from Easter to October on Sundays, Wednesdays and Saturdays 2–5.30 p.m.

RHUDDLAN

A Norman castle was built here, on the mound, in 1073, but the present ruined castle is the work of

Rhuddlan is 3 miles south of Rhyl, 5 miles from

James of St George, military architect for Edward I. It was built in the five years between 1277 and 1282. It came under attack while it was being built, but Rhuddlan was used to such matters and beat off the attackers. An astonishing feat for the time was the diversion of the River Clwyd for two miles, which gave access to the castle for sea-going ships.

In spite of its strength, Rhuddlan had a stormy time in the early years but it held out. It also successfully resisted Owen Glendower in 1400, though he sacked and burnt the town. In the Civil War it was held by the Royalists until 1646. It was heavily slighted but is now well maintained. The visitor may obtain a good idea of what it was like in its great days.

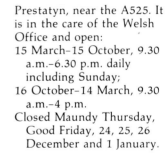

Prestatyn, near the A525. It is in the care of the Welsh Office and open:
15 March–15 October, 9.30 a.m.–6.30 p.m. daily including Sunday;
16 October–14 March, 9.30 a.m.–4 p.m.
Closed Maundy Thursday, Good Friday, 24, 25, 26 December and 1 January.

Rhuddlan

RUTHIN

Ruthin was originally an Edwardian castle, dating from 1277, and apparently of concentric design. It was the scene of a personal feud between Lord Grey, the then owner, and Owen Glendower in 1400. Grey had apparently been trying to acquire Glendower-owned lands by trickery, and when Glendower led his uprising Grey was an early target. However, although Glendower burnt the town he captured neither Ruthin Castle nor Grey. Two years later he took Grey prisoner and held him until an enormous ransom had been paid. In the Civil War, Ruthin was besieged by Parliamentary forces and, when it fell, was heavily slighted.

Ruthin Castle is just south of the town of that name. It is now a hotel, but visitors may inspect the ruins in the grounds. Ruthin now stages medieval banquets, and through them an impression of medieval food and life may be obtained.

DYFED

Dyfed contains both the most English part of Wales – for the former Pembroke-shire used to be known as Little England – and some of the most fervently Welsh as in the former Cardiganshire. Some of the great stones used to build Stonehenge in Wiltshire are said to have come from the Prescelly Mountains, near Fishguard. Dolaucothi, near Pumsaint (off the A282), was the site of the gold mines from which the Romans sent gold to the mints at Lyons and Rome. The old workings and aqueducts are open to visitors 10 a.m.–4.30 p.m. on weekdays.

ABERYSTWYTH

Little remains of what was one of the great castles of Edward I; it is difficult to believe that this was once more powerful than Harlech.

The area was important strategically in the distant past, and there is a large Iron-Age fort near by. Gilbert de Clare built a castle here in the twelfth century, and it saw plenty of action during the next hundred years. Edward I rebuilt it as part of his massive chain of castles to hold down the Welsh, but a hundred years later in 1404 it was captured by Owen Glendower. It changed hands twice before the English regained it. It was finally dismantled very thoroughly by Cromwell at the end of the Civil War. Silver was mined near Aberystwyth in the seventeenth century, and a mint was set up in the castle. Coins from it may be seen in the local museum.

Aberystwyth's extensive ruins, easily found on the sea-front, should not be missed. The corporation has now turned the site into a public park, with free admission.

CAREW

Although a castle was begun in the eleventh century, the present buildings are thirteenth and fourteenth century and were much improved in Tudor times. The interiors have great elegance. Carew is a friendly castle and is undoubtedly haunted; legend has it that a ghost is Sir Roland Rhys who is followed by his tame ape, which killed him. A more pleasant ghost is Nesta, an extraordinarily beautiful Welsh princess, who had an illegitimate child by Henry I but was not particularly mean with her favours. In her various marriages she helped found three famous families.

Carew is 4 miles east of Pembroke along the A4075, on which you will see a turning marked. It is open from April to September, Mondays to Saturdays 10 a.m.–6 p.m. Entry to the castle involves borrowing a key in the village (anyone will point out where) and traversing two roughish, often muddy, fields. That done, you are in an extraordinary castle.

CARREG CENNEN

Carreg Cennen is perched on a limestone crag above the River Cennen, and is often described as an eagle's nest. It was immensely strong, but occasionally fell, though not from frontal attack. It held out for twelve months against Glendower in 1403–4. Fifty years later it was the headquarters of bands of robbers and had to be reduced. Fortunately it was repaired later by the Earls of Cawdor into whose possession it came. Today, it has a weird grandeur; few castles are more impressive. You may walk along a dark passage within the walls to the cave – if you are feeling adventurous.

Carreg Cennen is 2½ miles south-east of Llandeilo and 4 miles north-east of Ammanford. It is in the care of the Welsh Office and open:
15 March–15 October, 9.30 a.m.–6.30 p.m. daily including Sunday;
16 October–14 March, 9.30 a.m.–4 p.m.
Closed Maundy Thursday, Good Friday, 24, 25, 26 December and 1 January.

CILGERRAN

The castle was built by Gerald of Windsor, whose wife Nesta (*see* Carew Castle) had been abducted by Cadwgan of Powys from an earlier castle on this site. Its valuable strategic position on the left bank of the River Teifi caused it to be attacked on many occasions. It escaped being involved in the Civil War, but fell into decay and was much ruined until the National Trust acquired it in 1930 and the Department of the Environment restored it. Note the clever tactical positioning of the drum-towers which dominate the entire perimeter. A very romantic picturesque spot, much beloved by painters.

Cilgerran is 2 miles south of Cardigan and the entrance is by a lane. It is in the care of the Welsh Offhce, and open:
15 March–15 October, 9.30 a.m.–6.30 p.m. daily including Sunday;
16 October–14 March, 9.30 a.m.–4 p.m.
Closed Maundy Thursday, Good Friday, 24, 25, 26 December and 1 January.

Cilgerran

overleaf—Kidwelly

KIDWELLY

Kidwelly Castle was built by Roger, Bishop of Salisbury, at the beginning of the twelfth century. Bishops were very martial in those days although not permitted to carry a sword; however, they carried other, equally lethal, weapons. The castle changed hands several times in the next century and was occupied more by the Welsh than the English. It was extended and improved at the end of the thirteenth century and beginning of the fourteenth, by which time it had become Crown property. It was in action again when Glendower attacked it in 1402, and was damaged but subsequently repaired.

Kidwelly is 8 miles south of Carmarthen, on the A384 (Carmarthen–Llanelli). It is in the care of the Welsh Office and open:
15 March–15 October, 9.30 a.m.–6.30 p.m. daily including Sunday;
16 October–14 March, 9.30 a.m.–4 p.m.
Closed Maundy Thursday, Good Friday, 24, 25, 26 December and 1 January.

LLANSTEPHAN

There were fortifications here in the Iron Age, but the first castle (probably of wood) was built by Gilbert de Clare in 1112. It changed hands many times, often by fighting but sometimes by legal wrangles. It was captured by Glendower in 1403, but subsequently retaken. In the nineteenth century it fell into very poor repair, but has now been much restored. Although a ruin, it is a memorable castle to visit and many paintings and sketches have been made of it.

Llanstephan is 7 miles south-west of Carmarthen along the B4312. It is in the care of the Welsh Office and open:
15 March–15 October, 9.30 a.m.–6.30 p.m. daily including Sunday;
16 October–14 March, 9.30 a.m.–4 p.m.
Closed Maundy Thursday, Good Friday, 24, 25, 26 December and 1 January.
Visitors will do well to ascend by the circular path, for the steep bank, although shorter and thus inviting, tends to be slippery.

MANORBIER

Manorbier is extremely beautiful and well kept. It is also the castle of Gerald of Wales, or Giraldus Cambrensis, who was born here in 1146 and who was educated in Paris and Italy. Gerald came of the de Barri family, who were well-known in South Wales and also in Ireland, but Giraldus's principal fame comes from his *Itinerary of Wales*. In this he described Manorbier and life in Wales in his day,

Manorbier is 5 miles east of Pembroke along the B4585. It is open to the public from April to September 11 a.m.–6 p.m., and is a most rewarding castle to visit.

and the book is full of excellent descriptions and amusing anecdotes. In the castle there is a room refurbished to look like the room in which he wrote, and with a lifelike figure of Giraldus himself.

Manorbier Castle was besieged and captured by Parliamentarians in the Civil War, but was not slighted. Today it offers a remarkable insight into the more pleasant side of medieval life.

PEMBROKE

Pembroke has had an eventful history. It was begun in 1090 by Arnulf of Montgomery to control Pembroke river and Milford Haven. Its first castellan, Gerald of Windsor who married Nesta (*see* Carew Castle), was besieged by Cadwgan who had decided to starve him out. Gerald threw pieces of pig at them to show how well stocked he was. A story of a similar bluff is recounted of Carcassonne in southern France. In 1138 the 1st Earl built the great keep which is 100 feet high and has walls 19 feet thick at the base. It is astonishing in that it has neither buttresses, vaulting, nor arcading, yet is covered with a stone dome.

Pembroke held out against Glendower, but its greatest time was in 1648 when it stood a six-week siege and fell only through a combination of starvation and treachery. It was slighted but, in the nineteenth century, its then owner, Mr J. R. Cobb, made many repairs. There is much to see – and wonder at – at Pembroke. Among other attractions, there is a museum.

The castle is on the western edge of the town and its tall keep makes it easily visible from a distance. It is now in the care of the Pembroke Borough Council and is open in the summer 10 a.m. –8.30 p.m. and in winter 10 a.m.–dusk. Sunday opening times are half an hour shorter.

Pembroke

GWENT

Gwent is for many the first sight of Wales as they come in on the M4 and see Chepstow. Here, if they have a mind, they can take Offa's Dyke path and walk through some very picturesque scenery all the way to Prestatÿn in North Wales (a distance of 170 miles). The countryside with its woods and valleys will appeal more to the modern visitors than to the Romans who were so often ambushed here when they established their camp and amphitheatre at Caerleon (still very well preserved). The ruins of Tintern Abbey must not be missed, nor the River Usk, whether fishing is your hobby or not. There are the remains of many small fortifications, some of unknown date and uncertain origin. Note the fortified bridge at Monmouth – there are not many like it – the town where Henry V was born.

ABERGAVENNY

Abergavenny was the foremost of a strategic pattern of castles (Whitecastle, Grosmont and Skenfrith were the others) carefully sited by the Normans to further the conquest of South Wales. Its builders had no illusions about the toughness of their task, although they relished it. The first castle was of wood and was built by Hamelin of Ballon in 1090, but it was soon replaced by stone. In the late twelfth century it came into the hands of the notorious de Braose family. William de Braose was also Lord of Bramber in Sussex and did not spend all of his time at Abergavenny. From this point the history of Abergavenny castle includes treachery, murder and adultery.

Near by was a minor but powerful local chieftain named Sitsyllt who held Castle Arnold, near Penpergym. Sitsyllt was brother-in-law of Rhys ap Gruffyd, the Prince of South Wales, and had fought successfuly against Hamelin's descendants. William de Braose invited Sitsyllt and some others to Abergavenny on the pretext of delivering a royal message, then murdered them. De Braose then raided Castle Arnold where he killed Sitsyllt's son. It may take time to avenge a grievance but it takes even longer to forget it. In 1182, years after the murder, Sitsyllt's relations captured Abergavenny by scaling the walls and took their revenge. De Braose, however, was not there. De Braose later fell foul of King John (but not for his crimes), and had to flee to France. John captured de Braose's

The remains of this once great and powerful castle are at the southern end of the town, near the A40. Open 9.30 a.m.–dusk; guidebooks on sale. Regrettably there is not much left to show its former great strength, but no one with a real interest in Welsh history and castles will want to miss it. The most notable feature was apparently the exceptionally high walls which were meant to keep out the agile Welsh; they did not always do so. Part of the walls remain and still look high, but they were once much higher.

Abergavenny

wife and son and starved them to death in a dungeon.

The de Braoses managed to regain the castle later, but their line came to an end when a grandson of William de Braose was caught having an affair with the wife of Prince Llewellyn ap Iorweth. Llewellyn executed him promptly.

In 1402 the castle narrowly missed being destroyed by the local townspeople; the following year it was lucky to escape capture and destruction by Owen Glendower.

Its end came in 1645 when Charles I decreed it must be demolished to prevent it becoming a Roundhead stronghold. Few castles have had such a continuously violent existence.

CALDICOT

The castle dates from the twelfth century and in its day was clearly very large and strong. However, it was allowed to fall into ruin – though impressive ruin – until restoration was made recently.

Caldicot is 4½ miles from Chepstow on the B4245. It is open to the public from April to September on weekdays 1.30–4 p.m. and on Sundays 2.30–7 p.m.

CHEPSTOW

The castle was begun by William FitzOsbern in 1070, but his son lost it in an unsuccessful rebellion against William the Conqueror. Later it went to the Clare family, one of whom founded the nearby Tintern Abbey (not to be missed). Richard de Clare, 'Strongbow' the conqueror of Ireland, came from here. In the Civil War it was battered into submission by heavy guns in 1645, but was again garrisoned by Royalists, and again battered to surrender in 1648. Subsequently it had several owners and fell into ruin, but is now in excellent order. Note the figures on the roof – a form of deception target.

Chepstow Castle is on the west bank of the Wye, in the town itself, just off the A48. It is in the care of the Welsh Office and open:
15 March–15 October, 9.30 a.m.–6.30 p.m. daily including Sunday;
16 October–14 March, 9.30 a.m.–4 p.m.
Closed Maundy Thursday, Good Friday, 24, 25, 26 December and 1 January.

GROSMONT

Although a ruin, Grosmont is still very interesting, and in its day was very important militarily. It was built in the thirteenth century though, of course, added to later. Henry III came here in November 1233, with his wife, to strengthen morale against the Welsh, but Llewellyn put in a surprise night attack and captured a number of the King's retinue who were camped outside the castle. In 1405 it was besieged by Owen Glendower, but Prince Henry, later Henry V, relieved it. Grosmont, like its companions Skenfrith and Whitecastle, gives the visitor a very good impression of what life was like in a fighting castle in turbulent times. Many of the outworks, which made it strong, have disappeared, but you can still trace their outline.

Grosmont is on the B4347, 9 miles north-east of Abergavenny. It is in the care of the Welsh Office and open:
15 March–15 October, 9.30 a.m.–6.30 p.m. daily including Sunday;
16 October–14 March, 9.30 a.m.–4 p.m.
Closed Maundy Thursday, Good Friday, 24, 25, 26 December and 1 January.
A guide pamphlet may be obtained from the local post office, opposite the entrance to the castle.

PENHOW

The oldest lived-in castle in Wales and the home of the Seymour family. Guided tours.

Midway between Newport and Chepstow on the A48, 7 miles from the Severn Bridge. Open Wednesday to Sunday and Bank Holidays, mid-April to 30 September, 10 a.m.–6 p.m.

RAGLAN

The present buildings, ruined but well preserved, date from the early fifteenth century. It is large and its principal feature is the 'Yellow Tower of Gwent'. This is a hexagonal building, five storeys high, with each side 32 feet long. The walls were 10 feet thick. During the Civil War, Raglan was defended by the Marquis of Worcester and eight hundred men. He was seventy years old but conducted all operations himself and also paid the cost. The castle was besieged by Sir Thomas Fairfax with 3,500 Parliamentarians but it held out for a long time. It is said that the Marquis even used water-cannon with great effect.

Slighting the castle proved very difficult. More damage was done when some of the interior was removed to Badminton House, which also belonged to the family.

Raglan Castle is on the A40, halfway between Abergavenny and Monmouth, and 9 miles north-east of Pontypool. It is in the care of the Welsh Office and open:
15 March–15 October, 9.30 a.m.–6.30 p.m. daily including Sunday;
Closed Maundy Thursday, Good Friday, 24, 25, 26 December and 1 January.

Raglan

SKENFRITH

Skenfrith and Grosmont formed the base of a triangle of which Whitecastle (six miles east of Abergavenny) and Abergavenny were the apex. They might be considered as an arrow-head pointing into Wales. Skenfrith was established by William FitzOsbern (*see* Chepstow Castle), but at this period consisted only of a motte and a wooden tower. The present buildings all date from the early thirteenth century and their outstanding feature is the central tower which is 21 feet in diameter. This appears as if it were built on a mound, but in fact the ground was raised around its base. Apart from this formidable-looking tower, corner towers and a curtain wall, Skenfrith does not look very defensible. However, in its day it had a wide moat fed by the nearby River Monmow and was able to give a very good account of itself. It figured in the Welsh wars of the thirteenth century, but soon ceased to have any further military use. Today, it is a popular holiday resort.

Skenfrith Castle is 10 miles west of Ross-on-Wye, and 10 miles east of Abergavenny on the B4521. It is a National Trust property, but is cared for by the Welsh Office and open:
15 March–15 October, 9.30 a.m.–6.30 p.m. daily including Sunday;
16 October–14 March, 9.30 a.m.–4 p.m.
Closed Maundy Thursday, Good Friday, 24, 25, 26 December and 1 January.

WHITECASTLE

This is a compact, sturdy castle which was originally called Llantilio. Later it became Whitecastle from the external plaster, of which fragments remain. It is lovingly cared for by the Welsh Office – as indeed are all their castles – and by those who guard and work on them. Many craftsmen refuse more lucrative work because they get greater pleasure and satisfaction from the repair of ancient castles.

There is a lot to see at Whitecastle. There are high walls of the sort which once existed at Abergavenny, but no longer do; there is a very deep moat, there is even an oven.

Whitecastle is just what you would expect a fighting castle to look like. It was one of the Skenfrith, Grosmont, Abergavenny group, all of which were likely to come under sudden surprise attack.

6 miles east of Abergavenny, on the road to Ross. It is in the care of the Welsh Office and open:
15 March–15 October, 9.30 a.m.–6.30 p.m. daily including Sunday;
16 October–14 March, 9.30 a.m.–4 p.m.
Closed Maundy Thursday, Good Friday, 24, 25, 26 December and 1 January.

GWYNEDD

The castles of Gwynedd are unmatched anywhere in the world. They were built by Edward I in a determined attempt to subdue the Welsh by establishing a chain of castles in their remotest fastness. Some Welsh castles, such as Builth, Aberystwyth and Flint have largely or completely disappeared but here, along the Menai Straits which Edward set out to control, there remains a series of powerful, well-preserved and elegant castles. That they have lasted so well is certainly lucky because here, as elsewhere in earlier centuries, there have been attempts to demolish castles, either for political reasons or to put the stones to use in house building. Fortunately they have withstood these threats well.

BEAUMARIS

Beaumaris was the last of the great castles which Edward I built to hold the Welsh in subjection. It was begun in 1295 and took twenty-eight years to build. Its position enables it to control the north-eastern end of the Menai Straits. It was the last word in military sophistication of the day, a concentric castle with every device for making the way of the attacker hard and the life of the defender easy. It is also extremely beautiful and a most rewarding castle to photograph. It never had to stand a siege to test its capabilities, but in the Civil War it surrendered to the Parliamentarians when the Royalists had lost a battle near by. Note the powerful flanking towers and the narrow baileys, making it impossible to use a proper battering-ram (*see* Introduction). The town of Beaumaris is a very pleasant place in which to stay.

Beaumaris is on the B5109, on the coast of the island called Anglesey, no longer a county in its own right but still known as 'The Mother of Wales', because of its great output of food. The castle is in the care of the Welsh Office and open:
15 March–15 October, 9.30 a.m.–6.30 p.m. daily including Sunday;
16 October–14 March, 9.30 a.m.–4 p.m.
Closed Maundy Thursday, Good Friday, 24, 25, 26 December and 1 January.

Beaumaris

CAERNARFON (CAERNARVON)

The Romans had a fort here, but the first motte was raised by the Normans in 1090. The present magnificent castle – more impressive outside than in – was built by Edward I between 1283 and 1292. At today's values it would have cost £2 million. The aim was to secure Edward's grip on Wales by controlling the south-western end of the Menai Straits, just as Beaumaris controlled the north-eastern. Although the main part was completed, the whole work was not finished even forty years later. Like Conwy, Caernarfon Castle was part of a complex consisting of a principal fortress and a walled town. Militarily it is an admirable construction, for its design enabled a small garrison to fend off attacks by quite large armies. It was heavily engaged in 1403 and again between 1644 and 1646. At various times complete demoliton was seriously contemplated, but fortunately never attempted. Recently, many useful repairs have been made. Time and stamina are needed to get full value out of a visit to Caernarfon.

Caernarfon, where the A48, A4085, and A4086 all meet, is well known because of the Prince of Wales's Investiture in 1969 and that of his great uncle before him; there is an Investiture exhibition here, a collection of armour, and a museum of the Royal Welsh Fusiliers. The castle is in the care of the Welsh Office and open:
15 March–15 October, 9.30 a.m.–6.30 p.m. daily including Sunday;
16 October–14 March, 9.30 a.m.–4 p.m.
Closed Maundy Thursday, Good Friday, 24, 25, 26 December and 1 January.

Caernarfon

CASTELL-Y-BERE

A stronghold of Llewellyn ap Iorwerth but subsequently captured and rebuilt by Edward I. Four interesting towers.

7 miles west of Dolgellau; in the care of the Department of the Environment. Open always.

CONWY (CONWAY)

The town of Conwy is delightful, although there is much foreboding about proposed roads and bridges, and the castle is even more impressive than Caernarfon. It is a linear castle and from it extend the walls which encircled the town; the drum-towers on these are as formidable as the whole of many castles elsewhere. It is possible to walk along a good section of this wall.

Building operations were directed by a famous architect, James of St George. He had a work force of 1,500 at his disposal, but the rocky site made progress slow. The castle, with a barbican at each end, and eight circular towers in between, would have cost the equivalent of £3 million today at least. When we consider that it was built simultaneously with similar castles like Caernarfon, Builth, Aberystwyth, Flint, Rhuddlan, Harlech and Beaumaris, it leaves us astonished to think that such a national effort could be made while Edward I was still at war with Scotland and France. The Welsh are proud of these great castles, partly because they are now objects of great beauty, but also because their sheer strength was a tribute to the fighting qualities of the Welsh, whom they opposed. Occasionally they were captured by the Welsh themselves.

Until recently Conwy was spelt in the anglicised way as Conway. However it is spelt, the castle should not be missed. It is in the care of the Welsh Office and open:

15 March–15 October, 9.30 a.m.–6.30 p.m. daily including Sunday;

16 October–14 March, 9.30 a.m.–4 p.m.

Closed Maundy Thursday, Good Friday, 24, 25, 26 December and 1 January.

Conwy

CRICCIETH

Criccieth is a mixture of Welsh and English building, having been begun by Llewellyn the Great in the early thirteenth century and much added to under Edward I's castle-building project in the early fourteenth. An early governor was Sir Hywel of the Axe, a Welshman who was knighted for gallant service in the French wars. Welsh archers were a valuable part of the English army at Crécy and Poitiers, but it was unusual for men-at-arms to be knighted. The castle was captured by Glendower in 1404 and apparently damaged by fire; but it remained in use as a residence for many years.

Criccieth Castle is on the A497 between Pwllheli and Portmadoc. It is in the care of the Welsh Office and open:
15 March–15 October, 9.30 a.m.–6.30 p.m. daily including Sunday;
16 October–14 March, 9.30 a.m.–4 p.m.
Closed Maundy Thursday Good Friday, 24, 25, 26 December and 1 January.

DOLBARDAN

Set on a small rock, it is one of the more impressive wild ruins in the country. The site is said to have been a fortress since the sixth century, but the present masonry is no older than the thirteenth. It was essentially a Welsh castle, although at times held by English forces. After 1282 it ceased to be important strategically, and some of its materials were taken to be used in Carnarfon castle.

Dolbardan is 1 mile south of Llanberis, off the A4086. It is in the care of the Welsh Office and open:
15 March–15 October, 9.30 a.m.–6.30 p.m. daily including Sunday;
16 October–14 March, 9.30 a.m.–4 p.m.
Closed Maundy Thursday, Good Friday, 24, 25, 26 December and 1 January.

DOLWYDDELAN

The ruins of a rectangular thirteenth-century tower mark the birthplace of Llewellyn ap Iorwerth 'the Great' who reigned in Gwynedd from 1194 to 1240. He did much for Welsh unity, both as a soldier and a diplomat.

5 miles south of Bettws-y-coed on the A496. In the care of the Welsh Office and open:
15 March–15 October, 9.30 a.m.–6.30 p.m. daily including Sunday;
16 October–14 March, 9.30 a.m.–4 p.m.
Closed Maundy Thursday, Good Friday, 24, 25, 26 December and 1 January.

HARLECH

When Harlech was built between 1283 and 1290 the sea came up to the base of the crag on which it stands, but the sea is now half a mile away. Building the castle was an extremely difficult task and required an enormous labour force. The foundations had to be hacked out of solid rock, with primitive tools; the technique of splitting the rock with alternate heat and cold was laborious but essential. Once built, the castle was militarily so ingenious it could be held with a small force of thirty to forty men; it could always be relieved or supplied from the sea if the ships were available.

It was captured in 1404 by Owen Glendower, but it is not wise for a great guerrilla leader to tie himself to a fixed base. The castle was eventually besieged and captured by 1,000 men in 1409, by which time most of the garrison had died of starvation. Some of the massive stone cannon-balls used in the siege are on view. In the Wars of the Roses it sustained a seven-year siege, and the song 'March of the Men of Harlech', dates from this period. The future Henry VII was in the castle at the time of the siege, and the experience is said to have contributed to his parsimonious temperament. In the Civil War, it stood a year's siege.

The massive gatehouse is a castle in itself. Harlech is an excellent example of the ultimate development in sophisticated concentric castle-building, and the visitor can see all its assets very easily.

Harlech is on the A496 and is a striking sight as you approach it. It is in the care of the Welsh Office and is open:
15 March–15 October, 9.30 a.m.–6.30 p.m. daily including Sunday;
16 October–14 March, 9.30 a.m.–4 p.m.
Closed Maundy Thursday, Good Friday, 24, 25, 26 December and 1 January.

Harlech

MID GLAMORGAN

Mid Glamorgan contains much of Welsh industry and bears the scars of the past. The Rhondda valley is far from beautiful but the choirs which have come from that area show Welsh musical talent at its best. Welsh people tend to be gifted artistically and musically; that they combine artistry with athleticism is shown by their skill and success at Rugby Football. They are proud to have won the International Championship year after year in the last two decades but even prouder of the style and artistry of their player heroes. Welsh supporters are notably partisan but they are the first to applaud skill in an opponent. Their own teams invariably demonstrate it. If you wish to know why the English needed to build such strong castles in Wales, go and watch a Welsh Rugby Football match.

CAERPHILLY

Caerphilly was at one time the largest castle in Wales and is large by any standards. Although there was a fortification here in Roman times, the present castle dates from 1268 when Gilbert de Clare began building. Prince Llewellyn soon destroyed the first castle, but another was begun in 1271. The second castle, with its vast, ingenious water defences and numerous bastion towers, proved a harder nut to crack. The only enemies which had much effect on its structure were time and decay, although Cromwell ordered it to be slighted and the lakes drained. The lakes, of course, are artificial. From the slighting, one tower, 50 feet high, leans at an apparently perilous angle but it has been like that for over three hundred years.

The size and strength of Caerphilly – still obvious today – are a tribute to the fighting qualities of the Welsh, for it was built to hold them in subjection.

Caerphilly Castle is in the town itself, which lies 9 miles north of Cardiff. It is in the care of the Welsh Office and open:
15 March–15 October, 9.30 a.m.–6.30 p.m. daily including Sunday;
16 October–14 March, 9.30 a.m.–4 p.m.
Closed Maundy Thursday, Good Friday, 24, 25, 26 December and 1 January.

COITY

The castle was acquired, in 1120, by Payn de Turbeville, a Norman knight, apparently as the marriage dowry of Sybil Morgan, daughter of the owner. The story is mingled with some slightly improbable legend. The castle withstood a tremendous battering from Glendower's army in 1404, but held out. The owner at that time was Sir

Coity is 1½ miles to the north of Bridgend. The key is kept at a nearby cottage. The castle is in the care of the Welsh Office and open:
15 March–15 October, 9.30 a.m.–6.30 p.m. daily including Sunday;

Coity

William Gamage who was as warlike as his predecessors, the Turbevilles. Coity has a remarkable array of arrow loops and, although a ruin, has a lot to show to the visitor.

16 October–14 March, 9.30 a.m.–4 p.m.
Closed Maundy Thursday, Good Friday, 24, 25, 26 December and 1 January.

OGMORE

Ogmore is somewhat unusual in that it is approached over stepping-stones across the Ewenni river. The castle was originally built in the early twelfth century to guard this crossing-point and deny it to the unwelcome. There is also a convenient ford over the River Ogmore near by, and the castle holders controlled that too.

There are remains of a fine twelfth-century keep here, and other masonry. The castle seems to have had an uneventful history and to have fallen into ruin through neglect rather than warefare. It was, however, long used as a prison and the old courthouse may be seen.

Ogmore Castle is 2 miles south of Bridgend on the B4524. It is in the care of the Welsh Offie and open: 15 March–15 October, 9.30 a.m.–6.30 p.m. daily including Sunday; 16 October–14 March, 9.30 a.m.–4 p.m.
Closed Maundy Thursday, Good Friday, 24, 25, 26 December and 1 January. The keys are kept at the farmhouse facing the castle.

POWYS

Powys has the Berwyn Mountains to the north and the Brecon Beacons to the south. The Brecon Beacons include both a national park and a military training area of exceptional severity. Powys is the heartland of Wales. It is less rugged than most of the other regions.

BRONLLYS

Bronllys is an interesting small castle of which the remains, apart from earthworks, consist mainly of an 80 feet high tower. This was probably built in the twelfth century although William Rufus (1087–1100) is known to have used the site earlier on an incursion into Wales. There are few records of fighting at the castle, but the military activity in this area was unlikely to have been slight, merely unchronicled.

Bronllys is just off the A749 and is 7½ miles from Brecon. It is in the care of the Welsh Office and open:
15 March–15 October, 9.30 a.m.–6.30 p.m. daily including Sunday;
16 October–14 March, 9.30 a.m.–4 p.m.
Closed Maundy Thursday, Good Friday, 24, 25, 26 December and 1 January.

PAINSCASTLE

There is little masonry but there are good earthworks here. It was built around 1230 by Payn Fitzjohn and passed to the detested de Braoses. It was frequently the scene of fighting, but now all seems very tranquil.

4½ miles north-west of Hay-on-Wye. Open at all times.

POWIS

The origins of Powis are obscure and even the exact site of the first fortification is unknown, but there was a castle in the area in the twelfth century. English and Welsh fought bitterly for the castle, and it changed hands several times. In the Civil War it was held for the Royalists but captured by the Parliamentarians after a siege. It was not slighted.

Powis was almost completely rebuilt as a mansion-castle in the early eighteenth century. It was remodelled again later and has superb

Powis is on the outskirts of Welshpool. It is cared for by the National Trust, but the Earl of Powis lives here. It is open:
Easter Saturday, Sunday and Monday; then 1 May–28 September daily except Mondays and Tuesdays, 2–6 p.m.
Open on Bank Holiday Mondays 1–6 p.m.
Tea is available.

Powis

interiors. It came into the possession of the family of Clive of India in 1801, and there are many relics of Clive at the castle. The name Clive has now been dropped and that of Herbert, the original holders, is used as the family name. The castle is red sandstone; and it is surrounded by magnificent gardens.

TRETOWER

Tretower is a polygonal castle which was established by John Picard when the Normans, under Bernard de Neufmarché, were forcing their way up the Usk valley in the eleventh century. It is small and does not look particularly defensible, but the site is marshy and there is no doubt that in its day Tretower made good use of water and marsh to deter enemies. This did not prevent it changing hands several times in the Welsh wars, but it did manage to beat off attacks by Owen Glendower's forces; not many castles did.

Visitors to Tretower will not miss the restored manor-house, Tretower Court, near the entrance. Until a few years ago it was used as farm buildings but now its twelfth-century hall, its solar, and its other rooms, are much as they were many centuries ago. Henry Vaughan, the seventeenth-century poet, lived here.

Tretower is 3 miles from Crickhowell off the A479. It is in the care of the Welsh Office and open:
15 March–15 October, 9.30 a.m.–6.30 p.m. daily including Sunday;
16 October–14 March, 9.30 a.m.–4 p.m.
Closed Maundy Thursday, Good Friday, 24, 25, 26 December and 1 January.

SOUTH GLAMORGAN

Cardiff, the capital of Wales, is here, and apart from the castle there is much else of interest. The St Fagan's Folk Museum, off the B4488, open daily, gives a very good insight into rural Wales of the past.

CARDIFF

The Romans had a fort here, and at the end of the eleventh century the Normans built a motte in it. Robert, Duke of Normandy, son of the Conqueror and brother of Henry I, was imprisoned here for twenty-eight years. Some reports say he lived in comfort, others that he was blinded and dressed in rags. The Welsh captured the castle in 1158 and extracted handsome concessions for releasing their prisoners, the Earl of Gloucester and his family. The castle was extended and strengthened in the later Middle Ages, and was fought for by Owen Glendower and later, in the Civil War, by Parliamentary forces. Guided tours are conducted through the interior, which has been partly remodelled.

Cardiff Castle is close to the city centre, in Castle Street, and is owned by the corporation. It is open in March, April and October on weekdays 10 a.m.–12 noon, and 2–4 p.m.; from May to September it is open on weekdays 10 a.m.–12 noon and 2–6.30 p.m.; on Sundays it is open 2–5 p.m. It is closed from November to February.

CASTELL COCH

Castell Coch – the Red Castle – was originally built in the thirteenth century, but the present castle is entirely a nineteenth-century reconstruction from the original plans, with a Victorian interior and furnishings. It was built by a brilliant architect called William Burgess and financed by the enormously wealthy Marquis of Bute. It is quite incredible and not to be missed.

In the grounds there is said to be a vast treasure guarded by three ravens. Possibly!

Castell Coch is 5 miles north of Cardiff. Take the A470 and turn right in the village of Tongwylais – ¼ mile along the road will bring the visitor to the castle gate on the left. The castle is in the care of the Welsh Office and open:
15 March–15 October, 9.30 a.m.–6.30 p.m. daily including Sunday;
16 October–14 March, 9.30 a.m.–4 p.m.
Closed Maundy Thursday, Good Friday, 24, 25, 26 December and 1 January.

WEST GLAMORGAN

In West Glamorgan you are moving away from the industrial area, though there is still much of it to be seen. The Gower Peninsula is almost a little country of its own. Oxwich Castle is interesting, but is a sixteenth-century mansion, Pennard Castle, half a mile south of Parkmill on the A4118, is impressive but much reduced from its former magnificence.

OYSTERMOUTH

Built by the notorious de Braose family in 1280. An impressive square keep, and a banqueting-hall. Plenty to see but you might not see the ghost of the White Lady whose room is here.

On the A4067 at the Mumbles, 4 miles south-west of Swansea. Open May to September, 12 noon–8 p.m.

WEOBLEY

Weobley is a small castle and sometimes described as being a fortified manor-house. If it were such, it was a very sturdy example. Its main interest for us is that even in ruins it shows how people lived in former times, and how their rooms related to each other.

Weobley Castle is on the north coast of the Gower Peninsula. It is maintained by the Welsh Office and open:
15 March–15 October, 9.30 a.m.–6.30 p.m. daily including Sunday;
16 October–14 March, 9.30 a.m.–4 p.m.
Closed Maundy Thursday, Good Friday, 24, 25, 26 December and 1 January.
(There are remains of another Weobley Castle in the county of Hereford and Worcester, but only earthworks remain there. Both are pronounced 'Webley'.)

Weobley

APPENDIX

Dining and sleeping

As mentioned elsewhere in the book, you may stay in great comfort in various castle hotels: Lumley in Durham, Taunton in Somerset, and Ruthin in North Wales are examples. For those travelling around, there are numerous small hotels and bed-and-breakfast establishments. For those who like to obtain their security and comfort in advance, the following list of hotel groups might be useful:

Thistle Hotels, 111 Holyrood Road, Edinburgh. Telephone, 0632 21073. The group has hotels in most parts of Scotland and some parts of England.

Grand Metropolitan Hotels, Stratford Place, London W1A 4YU. Telephone, 01–629 6618. The group has hotels all over Britain.

Trust Houses Forte, 71 Uxbridge Road, London W5. Telephone, 01–567 3444. The group has hotels all over the country, many of which have been modernised without spoiling the original appearance.

Embassy Hotels (Allied Breweries), 107 Station Street, Burton-upon-Trent, Staffordshire, run occasional castle weekends when a number of castles are visited and discussed.

Best Western Hotels, 26 Kew Road, Richmond, Surrey, TW9 29A. Telephone, 01–940 9766.

Medieval banquets may be found at Caldicot (Gwent), Lumley (Durham), Seaton Delaval (Northumberland), and Chilham (Kent). At Thornbury (Gloucestershire) you eat modern food of the highest quality. Everywhere you have to book in advance.

How to find them

Most of the listed castles are easy to find. A motorists' road map is usually adequate for tracking down castles, but a 1:50,000 Ordnance Survey map is better if you are prepared to go to the expense. However, many people feel that the previous one inch to the mile series (1:63,000) is better, as well as cheaper, so if you have a stock of these, or can buy them cheaply, they will do as well. Finding one's way about the countryside has been made considerably more difficult by the provisions of the recent Local Government 'Reform' Acts, which created enormous administrative complexities, and changed many of the old county names. Where it might be helpful we have given the grid references from the Ordnance Survey Maps.

Opening times

The opening times of the castles in this book are given next to the description. They were correct at the time of going to press and have been checked against any future changes. However, changes are made from time to time. Occasionally castles in the care of the Department of the Environment, Scottish Office or Welsh Office may be closed for one day a week owing to staff shortages.

In order to make absolutely sure that a journey will not be wasted, readers might care to telephone Area Offices to check that all will be as expected on arrival.

North   0228 31777

Yorkshire and Lancashire	0904 22902
Midlands	0702 765105
East Anglia	0223 358911
South-East	0892 24376
South-West	0272 44061
Scotland	031 229 9321
Wales	0222 825111

It is now Government policy to try to standardise the opening times for all castles in official care whether administered by Department of the Environment or Regional offices. These times are given in the text. However, the difficulty of staffing castles in remote areas will be readily appreciated. Some castles may in the future be left open to visitors all the time, others may be closed at times when visitors are normally very few, such as on Sunday mornings. For the majority of castles the opening times listed should be reliable.

GLOSSARY

Adulterine Castles Castles built in King Stephen's reign in England (1135–52) without royal permission. Most were demolished by Henry II who followed him.

Allure A wall walk within the battlements.

Ashlar Square stone blocks used for facing walls.

Bailey Enclosure round the castle, also known as the ward.

Ballista Early crossbow or sling. Ballista comes from the Greek word ballo but the device has a number of other names.

Banquette A raised platform behind a rampart to fire from.

Barbican Outer defensive tower, usually sited ahead of the gatehouse.

Bastion A defensive projection. Sometimes it was a circular tower but it could be an octagon or mere square projection. Usually it facilitated flanking fire.

Beffroi or *belfry* A siege tower. Compare belfry in church towers; the word meant shelter and had no connection with bells.

Bergfried A tall thin tower often found in German and Austrian castles.

Bombard Early form of cannon.

Brace Low defensive platform to check attack on lower walls.

Brattice Wooden platform built out from battlements so that the defenders could drop missiles onto those below. Also known as hoardings and *brétaches*. Later replaced by a machicolation (*q.v.*).

Caltrop or *caltrap* Ball with four spikes used to obstruct cavalry.

Casemates Galleries built at the base of castle walls from which defenders could fire into the faces of surface miners and battering-ram parties.

Chat castel Bore or ram (literally; castle cat).

Chemise Outer curtain wall, also referred to as the bailey or even the *enceinte*.

Concentric A system of walls each enclosing the other. The inner higher walls were able to fire over the outer and give great concentration of missiles.

Crenellations Battlements. They were divided into merlons (stonework) and embrasures (spaces). The word *crenel* in Norman French meant a gap in the teeth. 'Licence to crenellate' meant permission to fortify.

GLOSSARY

Crow   A hook on a long pole which could be used for hooking on to battlements or snatching up unwary attackers.

Curtain   The outer wall around the bailey (see *chemise*).

Ditch   The fosse. A dry or wet moat.

Donjon   The original name for the main tower; it was a corrupted form of *dominus* meaning 'the master'. It was also known as the turris or tower and much later became known as the keep. As prisoners were kept in the lower and less salubrious portions, the word came to be applied to any dark, unpleasant, underground prison.

Drawbridge   A bridge which could take several forms. It could be raised by chains or tilted by levers.

Embrasure   Originally opening in parapet; later a gunport.

Enceinte   Another word for an outer curtain wall; as *chemise* or *bailey.*

Flanking   On the sides. Flanking-towers enabled archers to shoot along and parallel with the walls.

Garderobe   Latrine.

Gatehouse   Strongly fortified building over the main entrance (*see* Warwick and Denbigh castles).

Gunport   Gunloop. Opening for gun to fire through.

Hoarding   (*see brattice*).

Juliet   Circular donjon.

Keep   (*see also donjon*). A shell-keep was a wall built around the top of a mound with the buildings on the inside. The word keep was never used in medieval times.

Machicolation   Stone platform built out from battlements with holes in the floor for dropping missiles. Used mainly over gateways in Britain but employed much more widely elsewhere.

Malvoisin   Siege tower or assault mound (literally, 'bad neighbour').

Mangonel   Siege engine worked by torsion.

Merlon   Stone part of battlement, often pierced with arrow slits.

Meurtrière   Murder hole. Opening in wall of gatehouse through which pikes were thrust.

Mine   Tunnel under wall or building (*see* St Andrews Castle).

Moat   Corruption of motte (*q.v.*). It could be either dry or wet.

Motte   A mound. The word came from the Norman French word for turf. Mottes were more than a mere heap of earth; considerable skill went into their planning, even if impressed manual labour was used. They took many forms.

Oubliette   A dungeon where prisoners were starved to death.

Petrary   Siege engine.

Portcullis   A heavy grating which could be dropped into passages, closing them, and perhaps isolating attackers who would be assailed through *meurtrières* (*q.v.*).

Postern   Back door or means of escape, similar to *sallyport.*

Ringwork   A term used by archaeologists to describe a system of fortifications.

Sallyport   A hidden or secret opening from which to attack or escape.

Slight   To damage a building so as to make it indefensible.

Solar   Originally a raised floor in the hall: later a withdrawing room.

Trebuchet   Siege engine worked by counterpoise. It was the only siege engine to be invented in the Middle Ages, the others had all been used earlier.

Under-croft   Crypt.

Yett   Openwork iron door.

INDEX